Praise

'Sifu Alan Bagley is an accomplished martial artist, great teacher and friend to many. The fact that he followed his passion and found a way to help support his family and wider community is a testament to the commitment, clear thinking and determination he has applied in his life. His insights in this book will help many start a journey that helps them grow. You need to read this book and move forward in your life. There is never going to be a better time to start than today.'
   — **Michael Crump, Aiki-Jujutsu instructor**

'An inspirational, informative read that makes the reader reflect on their own experiences, outlook on life and training in the martial arts. The use of the martial arts as a motivational tool and a roadmap for success is second to none, without the writer influencing the reader as to which art to study.'
   — **Paul Couldrey, Wing Chun Sifu**

'Taking The Martial is a great insight into the mind of a great teacher. It explores the reasons you may start and benefit from martial arts. The book is well written and provides motivational words of wisdom from Sifu Alan Bagley. If you are looking into training in the world of martial arts, then this book is

for you… if you already are training and would like to further your understanding of what's needed to be successful and happy in your art, this book is for you. Highly recommend read.'
— **Charlie Sihota, Gracie Barra Jiu-Jitsu practitioner**

TAKING THE MARTIAL

Kickstart Your Confidence

ALAN BAGLEY

Re think

First published in Great Britain in 2022
by Rethink Press (www.rethinkpress.com)

© Copyright Alan Bagley

All rights reserved. No part of this publication may be reproduced, stored in or introduced into a retrieval system, or transmitted, in any form, or by any means (electronic, mechanical, photocopying, recording or otherwise) without the prior written permission of the publisher.

The right of Sifu Alan Bagley to be identified as the author of this work has been asserted by him in accordance with the Copyright, Designs and Patents Act 1988.

This book is sold subject to the condition that it shall not, by way of trade or otherwise, be lent, resold, hired out, or otherwise circulated without the publisher's prior consent in any form of binding or cover other than that in which it is published and without a similar condition including this condition being imposed on the subsequent purchaser.

Image credit: Copyright Shutterstock | ipunk kristianto

To my wife Emily, who has been an inspiration to me since the day we met. You have shown me that with consistency and dedication, we can all achieve so much more in our lives. Words cannot express what that means to me.

To my Mom. I know you were excited to see this book in publication so you could tell all your friends there is an author in the family. Although you didn't get the opportunity to see the finished book, I want you to know that you will be forever in my heart.

Your loving son

Contents

Introduction		**1**
	The many benefits of martial arts	4
1	**Planning Your Journey**	**7**
	What is a martial art?	8
	Yin Yang	10
	Seek out inspiration	12
	Action equals change	16
	Summary	18
2	**The Hidden Benefits Of Martial Arts**	**21**
	The importance of consistency	22
	Health benefits	24
	Managing stress levels	28
	Additional focus	30
	Other benefits	31
	Summary	34

3	**It's All In Your Mind**	**37**
	Overcoming limiting mindsets	38
	Investing in yourself	42
	Measurable results	44
	Summary	46
4	**Martial Arts Styles**	**47**
	Hard and soft martial arts techniques	50
	The hard style	53
	Mixed martial arts	54
	Summary	56
5	**The Right Martial Art For You**	**57**
	Chinese martial arts	58
	Japanese martial arts	60
	Korean martial arts	62
	Brazilian martial arts	63
	Body and mind	65
	Summary	69
6	**Personal Growth And Development**	**71**
	Martial arts and positive change	72
	Developing discipline	74
	Summary	76
7	**Find The Right School**	**79**
	Do your research	80
	Your first session	84
	Empty your cup	89

	Going the distance	94
	Summary	96
8	**Investing In You**	**99**
	Forming habits	100
	Overcoming barriers	105
	How martial arts empower you	110
	Summary	114
9	**Laying The Foundations**	**115**
	The four stages of learning	116
	Building a solid foundation	120
	Repetition is the mother of skill	124
	Quality over quantity	127
	Summary	130
10	**Advance In Your Art**	**133**
	The route to advancement	133
	Breathing and meditation	136
	Body conditioning	138
	Practise your forms	139
	Summary	141
11	**Martial Arts In The Modern Age**	**143**
	Fight, flight or freeze	145
	Scenario-based training	148
	Discipline, respect and responsibility	150
	Summary	155

Conclusion	157
Acknowledgements	165
The Author	167

Introduction

Working over the years with hundreds of students of all shapes and sizes, and varying ages and abilities, I have seen again and again the power of traditional and hybrid martial arts to impact lives. Positive changes in fitness, confidence and understanding of self are only a small part of what you can gain when you train in martial arts. These gains are available to anyone, whatever their age, fitness level, gender or race.

I've seen people inspired and transformed. With guidance and encouragement, they become more capable in all aspects of their lives. I have watched children and adults flourish, grow and become more agile, self-confident and successful. I've had feedback from students and parents who are amazed to see the difference in their own or their children's attitude, confidence and ability. Young adults attain a new level of maturity, respect and discipline. As students progress, becoming more adaptable and knowledgeable, and share their knowledge with new members, they not only gain a sense of value, they cement their understanding of the art.

My journey into martial arts began with kickboxing. In the late 1980s, the choice in martial arts was minimal, karate or kung fu being pretty much it unless you lived in London. There has always been a more diverse variety of clubs and styles in the south of England, like ninjutsu, for instance. Who wouldn't want to train to be a ninja?

It was my friend Steve who persuaded me to try a recently opened martial arts school in Birmingham's city centre; an idea I found so exciting. I had spent many years practising football, ice skating and golf (badly) with friends, so I was intrigued as to what the martial arts had to offer. Was it really like the movies?

It is always nice, the buzz of starting something new, the anticipation of a first lesson. The school was in an old converted factory unit that had seen better days. There were worn carpets on the floor, broken mirrors around the walls, and it had an odour that is difficult to describe but will be forever in my memory.

INTRODUCTION

After two hours of training and a kick to the groin (I knew I should have purchased a groin guard), my love for martial arts was cemented. The buzz of training, the physical and mental challenges – it was like a drug and I couldn't wait until the next session. I was well and truly hooked and it's been my passion ever since.

However, my martial arts journey nearly didn't even begin. In any journey, there will always be bumps in the road, twists and turns, and for me, a major obstacle blocked my way right at the start.

At that point in my life, I was studying the Bible. I didn't think for one moment that learning a martial art would have any bearing upon my religious studies. How wrong I was. Pressure came from all sides to give up my martial arts dream. 'A child of God should not practise violence' was something I heard regularly, born out of ignorance and a lack of understanding.

The ability to defend myself or my loved ones from a violent encounter is something I take very seriously, so the pressure to give up my passion caused great internal conflict, a huge weight on my mind. I had a decision to make, one that would shape the rest of my life, and only I could make it.

The choice I made has given me the best job in the world.

The many benefits of martial arts

If I were to say the words 'martial artists' to you, what would be the first thing that springs to your mind? Would it be a famous movie star like Bruce Lee or Jackie Chan? Would it be a mixed martial artist like Conor McGregor? Maybe it would be people in the park at sunrise, going through the slow and methodical movements of tai chi before the rest of the city is awake. You may conjure up scenes in your mind of someone performing violent, aggressive kicks and punches: egotistical men out for trouble, fighting anyone who looks at them in the 'wrong way'.

Many people have a preconceived idea of what martial arts are and what they can offer. This limited understanding usually comes from watching movies or talking to friends. No matter what the words 'martial arts' mean to you, the aim of this book is to give you an overview of what the arts really are and can bring to your life. I want to give you an insight into their benefits, expand your knowledge and introduce you into the amazing world of martial arts so you can begin or re-start your own journey. If you have never realised the benefits on both a physical and mental level that you can obtain from the martial arts, then this book is for you.

As an instructor with years of experience, I teach wing chun. I have seen my delivery of this martial art develop, adapt and progress, and my instructions have had a direct positive influence on hundreds of people's lives. Former students come up to me, shake my hand and tell me how much their personal life has changed for the better since they began studying martial arts with me.

As if that weren't enticement enough, learning a martial art has more benefits than just improved physical and mental health. Could martial arts be the journey that is missing from your world? What positive impact could it make? More *motivation* and a better *attitude*? More insight and a greater understanding of why *repetition* is essential in all aspects of your life? The importance of giving yourself *time* and *investing* in yourself to *advance* your knowledge and skills? There is always something new to *learn* when you study MARTIAL arts.

1
Planning Your Journey

A compelling reason *why* to do something will always beat *should*. Most people know they should exercise more, drink more water and less alcohol, and get better-quality sleep, but it doesn't mean they will.

Tapping into motivational factors and giving yourself a compelling reason to embark on a new journey in life makes you much more likely to succeed. Without a compelling reason why, 'should' will never be good enough. You have to have a why. If you don't then the excuses will soon mount up and you'll find yourself using them to not continue. They're not valid; they're just excuses, and one I hear time and time again concerns age.

Depending upon your current life circumstance, including your age, the thought of beginning a martial arts journey could be a little daunting, especially if you have never trained in the martial arts before.

It is a common misconception that you have to begin martial arts training as a child to gain maximum benefit. There are plenty of adults who get as much if not more from martial arts than the younger ones. Whatever your age, there's no need to worry; martial arts can be right for you. At the time of writing, a ninety-four-year-old is still active in aspects of teaching and training in the wing chun kung fu system. If a man of ninety-four can be active in his martial art, then age is no excuse.

Learning martial arts has the potential to transform your life in many ways. The benefits it brings will positively impact you, your family and your whole outlook. The first step in your journey is understanding the motivation you need to see it through. This chapter will give you a clear understanding of what and who can inspire you and the reasons *why* to take up the study of martial arts.

What is a martial art?

Martial arts are learned for many reasons: combat sports, self-defence, competition fighting or training for law enforcement or the military. As a young lad,

I often enjoyed watching martial arts in the movies, although looking back, I was more Cobra Kai than Mr Miyagi.

My outlook on the value of martial arts changed after I witnessed a fight in the school playground between two 'friends'. The speed at which the fight was over was an eye opener, albeit on a superficial physical level. This altercation made me re-evaluate martial arts. Seeing someone in real life moving like a movie star had me in awe.

As a young man, I got into thinking about this re-evaluation. Was this really what martial arts was all about? If I learned a martial art, would I be ready to take on the world?

Reviewing the fight now with more maturity and life knowledge, I understand that a real martial artist would have tried to de-escalate the situation and walk away. Physically engaging with someone can only be a last resort, if your life or physical wellbeing is in danger. Making the right decisions at the right time is just one of the many life lessons a martial art will teach you. You learn a lot about yourself and your ego when on a martial arts journey. Only the ego wants to get involved in a physical altercation when it thinks it has been insulted or wronged in some way.

Martial arts are so much more than the physical. Throughout the course of your life, problems will occur. Struggles, both physical and mental, will be a challenge to overcome. Of course, there will always be health issues that require hospitalisation or professional intervention, but training in a martial arts helps eradicate lack of motivation and negative self-talk and build self-worth. It guides you to focus on the task in hand rather than getting waylaid by other thoughts, just like daily meditation helps calm your mind. If you have had a stressful day, training even for a short period can give you the mental break you need to ease your stress and help you recharge.

Yin Yang

One aspect of martial arts that can be a stumbling block for a few people, especially if they have a religious background, is the Yin Yang symbol. Just because Yin Yang has roots in Taoism/Daoism, a Chinese religion and philosophy, this does not mean those participating in a martial art are following that religion. If you practise a religion that is important to you, there is no conflict of interests if you also want to practise a martial art.

Let's break the symbol down to look at the principles and philosophy behind it. The Yin Yang principles are woven into everyday life. If one side were to exist without the other, our lives would be unbalanced. It's the same with the martial arts. The use of the symbol is integral to these arts.

Yin Yang symbol and wing chun logo

If you look at the circle in the image, you will see a light swirl with a little dark circle within it, and on the opposite side, a dark swirl with a little light circle within it. The main circle represents the classic Yin Yang symbol. If we split the Yin Yang symbol, we would have two halves of the whole, one light, one dark, both with a small element of the other.

The darker swirl, Yin, is associated with hardness, negativity, coldness, wetness, depth, weakness, submission, intuition. The light swirl, Yang, is associated with softness, positivity, warmth, dryness, upward seeking and restlessness. If you were to live your life in one or the other side of Yin Yang, you would definitely notice an imbalance. Focusing on one side would not be beneficial, but if you put the two sides together to make a whole, then you have balance. Surely balance is what we are all after in life.

You cannot have Yin without Yang, or vice versa. The night will always follow day; what goes up must come down. There's left and right, hard and soft, hot and cold, positive and negative. Yin Yang forms a dynamic system of two halves that are complementary rather than opposing. When put together, the whole is greater than the sum of the separate parts, adding balance between two opposites.

Seek out inspiration

Before you start on your martial arts journey, you're going to need some inspiration. True inspiration must come from within, but you can also look to experts in a particular field who have achieved what you want to achieve.

Probably the most famous martial artist and arguably the most inspirational was movie star Bruce Lee.[1] From a young age to his unfortunate death, Bruce Lee faced prejudice and ridicule. He had to strive to achieve his goals, but he persevered to become one of the most revered martial artists of his era.

Bruce was born to Lee Hoi-Chuen and Grace Ho on 27 November 1940, in San Francisco, California. His father was a well-respected star of the Hong Kong Cantonese Opera, his mother a member of the Ho-tung Bosmans, an influential family in Hong Kong. A nurse gave the baby boy the name Bruce at the Jackson Street

---

1   Facts taken from the Bruce Lee website https://brucelee.com/bruce-lee, accessed 2 April 2021

Hospital, but he never used it until he entered secondary school and began studying the English language. Until then, he was known as Li Jun Fan.

When Bruce was three months old, the family returned to Hong Kong. This was when the immigration documents revealed that Grace Ho identified her mother as British. This seemingly insignificant fact would become one of the reasons why Bruce Lee experienced some difficulty being accepted in the Chinese community. There were those who shunned him because they believed he wasn't entirely Chinese.

Growing up, Bruce Lee often got into fights, but he had no formal training until the age of thirteen when he lost his first fight.[2] This loss led him to study wing chun with a master, even though some of the other students refused to train with him. Despite this setback, Bruce studied diligently and became proficient in the wing chun system.

Prejudice continued to haunt Bruce when he returned to America in April of 1959 and he was shunned by students when he studied drama and philosophy at the University of Washington. Bruce's passion for kung fu was one of the main reasons he studied philosophy – he wanted to delve into the philosophical underpinnings of martial arts

---

2   M Scott, *Bruce Lee, and Hong Kong's Infamous Rooftop Fight Clubs* (SBNation Bloody Elbow, 2019), www.bloodyelbow.com/2019/11/21/20951140/bruce-lee-and-hong-kong-infamous-rooftop-fight-clubs-kung-fu-martial arts, accessed 1 April 2021

techniques, and he used his kung fu knowledge to his advantage: he supported himself at university by teaching it.

When Bruce met Linda Emery, he would encounter even more prejudice and racism. For a Chinese man to date an American woman wasn't the done thing back then. Nonetheless, Linda Emery would later become Linda Lee when they married in 1964.

Bruce Lee went on to open up his first martial arts school, called Lee Jun Fan Gung Fu, in Seattle. When Bruce and Linda moved to Oakland, he opened a second school, but more challenges awaited him. Bruce was happy to teach anyone kung fu, but the other masters were not pleased about this. In 1964, he was challenged to a fight, the terms being that if Bruce was defeated, he would stop teaching non-Chinese people kung fu. He won the battle.

Bruce's struggles, attitude and determination are not only inspirational, but a testimony to his strength of character as a human being. Would he have been able to achieve what he did in his relatively short life if he didn't study martial arts?

Can you think of somebody who inspires you? Have you read a story or watched a movie that has motivated you? What positive effect did it have on your life?

Have you ever inspired anyone? Would you know if you had? Sometimes, people will watch from afar and take inspiration from the fact you are doing something they would like to do too. You never know who is watching and you don't need to be carrying out acts of derring-do; inspiration comes in many forms.

CASE STUDY – A REMARKABLE TRANSFORMATION

Zipporah trains with me and has undergone a remarkable transformation. Even though she is still young, the change in her has been impressive.

When Zipporah first came to my club, she wasn't attending because she loved martial arts; she didn't want to participate in the class at all. Her mum brought her to classes because she knew the benefits training would give her. Zipporah is bubbly with a beautiful smile and a polite manner, but back then she lacked confidence. She would fret about not mastering an exercise or technique correctly and often tried to get out of the classes if she could. I have to give credit to her mum, who used gentle encouragement to bring her to training consistently.

I had to be mindful when issuing instruction. Zipporah had been through some traumatic events at a young age and if I shouted an instruction too loudly, she would become fretful and tearful. Any sudden noises such as banging the pads together could be a trigger.

Over a few months of gentle guidance, her mum and I noticed subtle changes in her, both physically and in class participation, which was heart-warming to see.

Gone was the lack of confidence, the fretfulness, the fear of loud noises.

After around six months of training, the transformation was clear to see. If any new children came to class for a free trial, Zipporah was one of the first to greet them, ask their name, show them the facilities and explain the club etiquette. She helped them feel welcomed, and I didn't even have to pay her!

Two years into her training, Zipporah is the go-to person to demonstrate a technique or how to perform exercises correctly. She will happily stand in front of the class to do a warmup and she even volunteered to help in our mini martial arts programme. She is an inspiration all who meet her.

Action equals change

When we learn a new skill there will always be an action or a reaction; that action or reaction is change.

If you can cast your mind back to a time when you last learned a new skill or had to study a new subject and then applied that knowledge (action) what was the result? A new job, better career prospects?

If you have ever followed a fitness programme, learned new ways to train that action will ultimately lead to your body changing. So, learning plus action will always equal change.

PLANNING YOUR JOURNEY

Let's shine the spotlight back on you and your preparations for your journey into martial arts. How do you start? What changes will you need to make right away?

Small positive changes made daily will, over time, result in a significant improvement in your life. Try creating an action plan of simple daily exercises that you can add to your morning or evening routine. These small steps will accumulate to heighten your progress in any new discipline or skill you are learning, not just martial arts.

Taking time for yourself is equally important. The stresses and strains of the connected world mean we all tend to spend a lot of time on technology, be it messaging or calling on our mobile phone, checking social media and email on a laptop or watching TV. When was the last time you spent more than an hour of your time awake without checking your phone?

We all need something that disconnects us from technology and gives us time to invest in ourselves. If you join a martial arts school, the fact that you have committed to training helps to give you the incentive to attend each lesson. And over the space of a few short months, you will make progress, and that alone will likely be enough to encourage you even more.

A martial arts journey can be lifelong. There will be days when everything flows and you feel on top of the world. There will be other days when you're feeling frustrated, but think of a toddler learning to walk. They don't give up because they fail at first, so don't you give up either. Believe me, the rewards at the end will be great. Not only will you have mastered your body physically, but you will have a mental toughness and determination, confidence, self-esteem, thoughtfulness and discipline that you can apply to all kinds of situations.

Getting to the point of mastery in your journey is an outstanding achievement. Do you have the staying power to go from novice to master? Are you up for a challenge?

> **TASK**
>
> If you were to start your martial arts journey today, what would be your reasons why? Can you list five? Make sure they are compelling.
>
> How many friends or family members do you know who have studied martial arts? In what way have they inspired you?

Summary

In this chapter, we have looked at the importance of your reason why, and how only a strong reason to do a thing will keep you motivated. Simply knowing you should will never be good enough; you are much

PLANNING YOUR JOURNEY

more likely to succeed if you have a strong reason to do it. Having a why allows you to tap into the motivational factors that will keep you focused if things get tough and fully enjoy whatever it is you are embarking on, even the challenges.

Your martial arts training doesn't need to begin when you're a child for you to get the most out of it. There are so many benefits to be gained from the martial arts, one being understanding and controlling your ego.

The two sides of Yin Yang, integral to the martial arts, are woven into everyday life for balance. With some dedication, your martial arts journey can last you a lifetime, and who knows? You may end up becoming an inspiration to many others, just like Bruce Lee.

2
The Hidden Benefits Of Martial Arts

As well as the obvious benefits of studying martial arts, there are many less-obvious ones too. As long as you don't need healthcare from the professionals (and if you do, please be sure to get it), beginning a martial arts journey will be good for your health.

There is increasing evidence that the study of martial arts has a profound positive effect on your mental as well as your physical health.[3] Couple this with reducing stress, helping balance your mood and having obtainable goals, and the martial arts can shape and inspire you to become the person you truly want to be.

---

3   B Moore, D Dudley and S Woodcock, 'The effects of martial arts participation on mental and psychosocial health outcomes: A randomised controlled trial of a secondary school-based mental health promotion program', *BMC Psychology* 7, 60 (2019), https://doi.org/10.1186/s40359-019-0329-5

The importance of consistency

Cast your mind back to the last time you took on the challenge of learning something new. I am sure you would agree that effort, consistency and practice all played a vital role. If you want to change or develop a habit, you need to be consistent in your endeavour. This is vital for success.

Many children who attend my classes benefit from the consistency they learn from the study of martial arts. It provides focus, discipline, respect, loyalty and confidence that help develop a young person into a well-balanced, thoughtful individual. For children to grow healthily, they need nurturing. Sometimes they will offer resistance to the qualities they stand to gain from consistently studying and practising martial arts, but not giving in to their demands will benefit them in the long run. As a result, they will learn that if they persevere, things that were once difficult will become easy. Not everything in life will go their way, but they can overcome pretty much any obstacle with consistent dedication. What a great life skill to learn.

My mission for anyone who attends my school is to help them become a respectful, disciplined, dedicated individual and martial artist. I guide them to shape their life, thrive and take on the world, no matter their age.

CASE STUDY – OVERCOMING PERSONAL CHALLENGE

For some people, a challenge develops their determination and resolve. On one occasion, this happened for me in the shape of a press-up challenge. When I was a trainee, each week, one of the instructors would choose a student who they thought they could beat doing press ups.

These press ups weren't the regular up-and-down variety; they would be in high, middle and low starting and stopping positions. The challenges were often set to music, usually an extended 12-inch track lasting fifteen minutes. The goal was to do different press ups continually for the duration of the music.

This was my challenge. Press ups were something I really enjoyed doing and I was determined to win. One of my instructors at the time was the champion of the press ups. The gauntlet was thrown and the challenge made.

I never actually beat my instructor in this challenge, but I always gave him a run for his money. On many occasions, I was close to beating him, but his sheer will and determination were stronger than mine. Facing these challenges and enjoying the process helped to build my character and resolve, something that I will always be grateful for.

Health benefits

I'm sure you know that regular exercise brings with it health benefits. With martial arts, you gain stamina and endurance as well as mental focus, energy and an overall feeling of wellbeing. Some other physical benefits of taking up a martial art are cardiovascular health, increased muscle tone, weight loss and faster reflexes, along with more mobility, flexibility, strength, stability and coordination.

As with any new physical activity, the first few lessons will be the worst. I say 'worst' in the context of waking up the next day with aching and stiffness around your body, which is a sign that your muscles have been working harder than or differently to the way they are used to. Microscopic damage to the muscle fibres, resulting in the soreness or stiffness, is not something to be alarmed at. That said, please get any severe pain checked by a medical professional; here, I'm talking about the stiffness and aches that I'm sure you've all experienced at some time or another after trying out a new physical activity.

The mental health benefits of martial arts are often overlooked, but just a simple breathing exercise can lower your heartrate and stress levels and improve your mood. Thankfully, in the UK and across the world, the thinking around mental health is improving all the time. Talking about mental health issues is becoming increasingly acceptable and encouraged, but many people still don't get enough guidance. Practising a martial art can certainly help raise your mood.

CASE STUDY – HELP THROUGH HEARTACHE

When I had just started out on my teaching journey, I was conducting lessons under my instructor at his training facility. My role at the time was to introduce any new members to the wing chun system, explaining the importance of building a solid foundation and the role of the basics. Not the most glamorous of roles, but one I really enjoyed.

I had the pleasure of teaching a guy who was older than me. With plenty of life experience, although none at the time in martial arts, he would always bring a smile to my face with his little anecdotes. He was not very fit, though, and his flexibility needed improving. It was a good job that wing chun didn't require him to deliver any kicks above waist height – his words, not mine.

This guy didn't stay at the club long; four months maximum. When I realised he would not be returning, I remember thinking what a shame it was. We had built up a connection and he was a pleasure to work with.

Fast forward six years and I was at a friend's birthday party at a local social club. Just as I was leaving, I got a tap on my shoulder. It was this guy.

He was almost in tears as he explained that his leaving the martial arts club was to do with many family issues, ones totally out of his control. He went on to say that he was continuing the daily practices I had shown him and how this simple routine had helped with not only his physical health, but more importantly his mental health during this difficult time.

Six years earlier, little did I know the impact martial arts would have on his life.

Here are three questions for you to ponder:

- What does good mental health mean to you?
- Do you think there is still a stigma attached to discussing mental health issues?
- Would you feel comfortable discussing any mental health issues you have with another person?

Remember, your mental health is vitally important. It's just as important as your physical health. If mental health is defined by your state of wellbeing and the ability to cope with the stresses of day-to-day living, provide for you and your family and contribute to society and community, how many people do you think are in this state all the time?

As you continue your martial arts journey, your dedication will begin to spill over into your everyday life. You will become a calmer, more confident person. This subtle transformation is a by-product of both your physical and mental focus. By either mastering the technique or having the determination to continue even when you find a technique difficult, you will learn the importance of willpower and resolve.

Martial arts training embodies a moral values system that includes respect, character building, faithfulness and elevating to a better self. It provides physical and mental relaxation too, allowing you to control your mind and body and increase self-confidence.

If you are already training, next time you attend a class, be mindful of your mental health and how it will benefit. Also, bear in mind that your martial arts brothers and sisters may be dealing with issues you are not aware of. If you haven't yet begun your study of martial arts, keep this advice with you for when you do.

A short while ago, I asked three questions. Having read on, ask yourself the same questions again to see if you still answer in the same way.

CASE STUDY - YOU DON'T NEED TO GO IT ALONE

It is always refreshing when a couple starts training together, even if to begin with only one wants to train and the partner just comes along for moral support. This was the case with David and Jamie. David was initially the driving force behind wanting to train with me; Jamie in the beginning was a lot more nervous and unsure. Hats off to them both, but especially Jamie. Seeing someone who is out of their comfort zone learn the lessons and apply the actions, and witnessing the results is truly remarkable.

When they first started training with me, neither man was in the best physical health. They both knew they needed to lose a few pounds. Five years on, they look like completely different people. It is always heart-warming to look from the outside in and watch how people change, physically, mentally and emotionally; it's a reward I cannot put a value on. Their transformation is testimony to their dedication and hard work, and as a by-product, they have both become outstanding martial artists.

The personal growth and development of both of these men is remarkable. It has been my absolute pleasure to work with them, and long may this continue.

Managing stress levels

Everyone has a different understanding of stress because everyone experiences stress differently. If I were to ask you what things or situations stress you out, your answers wouldn't be the same as mine.

How do you define stress? For me, it's the degree to which you feel overwhelmed, unable to cope with any change that causes physical, emotional or psychological strain.

Many factors make up how you deal with stress, from the amount of sleep you've had to the time of day, whether you've eaten or simply the type of day you have had. These can have an effect on how you deal with any new pressure added to the mix.

Let's take an example. Imagine you've gone out for a drive and had a lovely day. The sun's been shining and you are happily singing along to your favourite songs when suddenly another motorist cuts in front of you, causing you to brake hard. You may react with angry words, but I am confident you won't let it spoil your day.

Now imagine the same drive, but your day has been very different. It's raining outside and you got soaked, you have just lost your job and the car radio isn't working. How do you think you would react in this instance to being cut up by the careless motorist? How anyone reacts to a situation depends up on their current mood and stress levels.

Did you know that a certain amount of stress is good for your body? For example, a cold shower is an external stressor, but experienced consistently and in moderation, this small amount of stress can have benefits to your overall mood and health. The cold water activates the sympathetic nervous system and boosts endorphins. When endorphin levels are high, you feel less pain and are more immune to the adverse effects of stress.

Attending martial arts classes can ease your stress levels a great deal. Not only will you be learning new skills and techniques, you will also learn coping strategies, including how to deal with stressful situations. Your inner calm will develop with every session.

As you build upon your knowledge in martial arts, daily practice of forms (a form is an individual training exercise) and stretching, along with breathing exercises, will fill your cup for the day and help you cope with the challenges life will throw at you.

Additional focus

'Discipline through action' is a phrase common in the martial arts environment. The premise behind the phrase is the process of learning through one specific activity – in this case, martial arts. This leads to better control and focus in other areas of life, be that study, work, social or hobbies.

You may set yourself goals when you begin your martial arts journey, such as becoming fitter, gaining your black belt or doing the splits. These goals will only be attained through the acquirement of new skills, which will require focus and attention.

Research has shown that martial arts training can enhance your focus and alertness, and the time spent practising the arts benefits cognition.[4] The study also indicates that the mental sharpness you gain is long term. This is because many of the martial arts techniques you will be learning will force you to solve complex problems while performing equally complex actions.

Other benefits

One of the fun things about learning a martial art is when you begin sparring and participating in partner work. These light contact drills are an excellent way to test out your skills on a live training partner instead of striking the air, pads or punch bags.

For some, the thought of partnering up to test their skills for the first time can be daunting. This feeling may worsen if you have observed the more senior students practising combat skills, but remember that they have many years of experience and use control in their sparring sessions. Getting involved with partner training and sparring is an essential step in your martial arts development, particularly if it takes you out of your comfort zone, something that is well-known to be an essential life skill.

---

4   P Douris, C Douris, N Balder, M LaCasse, A Rand, F Tarapore, A Zhuchkan and J Handrakis, 'Martial art training and cognitive performance in middle-aged adults', *Journal of Human Kinetics*, (2015), www.ncbi.nlm.nih.gov/pmc/articles/PMC4633263, accessed 3 May 2021

TAKING THE MARTIAL

Participating in partner work shows what areas – attack or defence – you need to improve. You will benefit significantly from this work and soon be looking forward to each lesson more than ever. As one of my senior students said, 'I couldn't find a better bunch of people to punch me in the face each week.'

Personal growth is a by-product of learning a martial art. You will explore and come to understand your strengths and weaknesses, likes and dislikes, both physically and emotionally. Psychologically, you will discover areas you need to develop.

In the wing chun kung fu system, the first empty hand form, meaning without weapons, is called siu nim tao, which means little idea or the way of the little idea. The form's concept focuses on the upper body's left and right sides using slow and steady movements while sitting in a low yee gee kim yeung ma (basic stance). This stance is designed to keep your legs engaged with muscles switched on. You are, in effect, relaxing the upper half of your body while simultaneously engaging your leg muscles, two opposite extremes.

The challenge, both physical and mental, is to perform the form slowly in a structured pattern, making small incremental improvements daily. Twenty minutes is the magic number to sit in yee gee kim yeung ma and complete the first section of the siu nim tao form.

There will be challenges in your martial arts journey which will differ depending on you as an individual and the martial art you are studying. Facing up to and overcoming these challenges will be part of your growth and personal development. Making connections in the classes you attend will help your journey and create new friendships. These friendships can grow and become a source of encouragement, both inside and outside your martial arts lessons.

Another great benefit of learning martial arts is variety. If you have been a regular gym attendee or runner, you'll know that the exercises can become a bit repetitive from time to time. When you attend martial arts lessons, each one will be different.

Everyone has areas in their life that need some attention, work or focus. This could mean making changes like getting more exercise or improving eating habits, drinking less alcohol, stopping smoking, avoiding procrastination or committing to yourself. These changes are all part of the self-discovery journey.

Commitment to the martial arts will not solve all your problems. What it will do is give you more life tools to help you become the person you truly wish to be.

TIP

When it comes to martial arts and self-defence training, it's good to remind yourself of this:

'I'd rather know it and not need it than need it and not know it.'

TASK

Write down five areas of your life where you believe that learning a martial art could benefit you and help with personal development.

Summary

This chapter has focused on the many hidden benefits of martial arts, but it's not an exhaustive list. The benefits you will gain from the study of martial arts will be individual and personal to you as a student, but we have looked at the most common ones, explaining how they can help you develop physically, mentally and emotionally.

When learning a martial art, you will experience lessons in overcoming personal challenges. Developing good habits will grow and strengthen your determination and resolve. Martial arts training embodies a moral values system including respect, character development, faithfulness and exerting oneself to do better.

THE HIDDEN BENEFITS OF MARTIAL ARTS

The additional focus that comes from martial arts study is a benefit that you can take into your everyday life. Couple this focus with things like goal setting and personal development, and you will notice subtle changes. Always remember, though, that training should be fun. Having fun and enjoying the process will relieve daily stress and help you unwind.

3
It's All In Your Mind

Understanding your mindset and the important role it plays in your martial arts journey is crucial. Now we've looked at seeking and gaining inspiration, exploring the Yin Yang philosophies, understanding your motivation to train in martial arts and the benefits the arts can bring, it's time to cover mindset.

Your approach to the learning process is paramount in any new endeavour. Learning a skill with the wrong mindset or belief will make the process difficult and unenjoyable, which in turn will make it more likely you will quit.

Overcoming limiting mindsets

What you are like as a person will affect your attitude and mindset to learning. If you think back to when you last had to learn something new, how did you approach the task? Was the skill difficult to master? Did you enjoy the challenge? If you didn't, it's likely you approached it with the wrong mindset.

Here are some examples of fixed mindsets that can hold you back from learning anything new.

Either I am good at something, or I'm not. If this resonates with you, I would like to ask you a few questions. How do you know you are not good at something if you never try? Do you hide behind this statement because you are fearful? How could you let go of that fear? Could you change the statement into something more positive?

An alternative mindset would be: I can always become better at something. All I need to do is practise.

What is the point of trying if I'm going to fail? Truth be told, yes, you could fail. You may fail ten, twenty or thirty times.

Is this what is holding you back? Are you fearful that you will put in a load of effort and still fail? Do you worry that people may laugh at you or be disappointed with your failings? Could you turn that fear on its head and, despite the possibility of failure, have a go anyway?

An alternative mindset would be: any loss or disappointment that I face allows me to reassess, reset and try harder next time.

I cannot learn anything new; I am too old. Advancing years do have their limitations, but is it really too late to become a learner? Think of all the resources you have at your fingertips. Since the birth of the internet, we have all had almost anything we want to learn accessible online, including the foundation of martial arts. I am sure you have seen plenty of instructional videos on YouTube, Vimeo and other streaming services.

An alternative mindset would be: I know what I want to learn, so I can learn it if I so desire, whatever my age. In fact, if the years are advancing, let's not waste any more time.

I do not like criticism. If you're averse to receiving criticism, it may be because of the way you've experienced it being delivered. If somebody is giving you constructive criticism and positive feedback thoughtfully and mindfully, take it on board and use it as motivation. However, if the person is harsh in their criticism, their feedback is not constructive and almost seems personal, this can be harmful. A good martial arts instructor will never resort to the latter, and nor will other students of the arts if they have been properly taught to respect their fellow beings, so the advice here is to choose your martial arts school wisely.

When you're receiving feedback, bear in mind that criticism is not a personal attack on you. Rather, it is intended to help you focus on the skillset you are learning. Even if you experience criticism that is harshly given, try to separate the negative words from the constructive intent to focus only on what is useful.

An alternative mindset would be: I will find value in any feedback I receive, no matter how harshly given, and focus on the constructive points.

If I see others doing well and I am not at that standard, I feel intimidated. Celebrating others' success while you are struggling with the same task can be difficult. Everybody is different and what comes easily to some may not for you.

Do not take it to heart if somebody succeeds when you are struggling. Embrace their success and use it to motivate you even more. The fact that they have achieved what you are striving to master shows that it can be done, so use that to spur you on even more. It's a reminder anything is achievable.

An alternative mindset would be: when I see others achieve and succeed, I will celebrate this, knowing it is something I can do too. If they can do it, so can I.

As a child, I was always told that I can't. This limiting belief is likely to have been instilled in you when you were young and your brain was more impressionable. If, when growing up, you were always told you can't do this or you are not smart enough to do that, or you're too big, too small, too fat, too thin, then it is bound to have an effect. Unfortunately, this baggage is something you will carry around with you until you question your beliefs about yourself.

An alternative mindset would be: my potential is only limited by me and my beliefs can be changed. I must discover for myself what I am truly capable of, so I will not listen to the opinions of others if their ideas are negative and critical.

There are many more examples of both negative mindsets and positive alternatives; the ones I have included are intended to show that for every limiting belief, there is a liberating belief. There is Yin and Yang.

If any limiting beliefs or negative mindsets that you are plagued by have sprung to mind while you've been reading this chapter, write them down and see how you can reword them to make them positive. This is a brilliant exercise for getting yourself into the mindset to succeed in any walk of life.

Investing in yourself

Any personal development programme takes time – time to embrace and learn new skills, habits and ideas. Faster is not always better, so prepare for the long term and learn to enjoy the process.

If someone were to say to you that you need to start investing in your future, what would spring to mind? Would it be financial investments, savings or buying a house? Would you think about your health as an investment? Investment in the martial arts encompasses physical, mental and emotional growth. As you progress in your journey, I would love you to get in touch via sifu@wingchunhalesowen.co.uk so that you can tell me about your personal adventure.

Life can be hectic, especially if you have a family. There always seems to be one more job to complete before you can get on with what you really want to do. Unfortunately, these jobs keep on coming, so you need to schedule time for yourself and stick to it. Otherwise, you will forever be chasing your tail. Committing to martial arts is giving yourself the permission and time to grow and change. It's investing in yourself.

Martial arts can almost be likened to a mentor. The fact that you schedule other parts of your life around your training is just one of many good habits that the arts will help you to get into. The additional discipline and focus you'll need to learn your forms or specific moves and drills will keep your cognitive functions ticking over. Training with like-minded people will give you an opportunity to make new friends and acquaintances. Your instructor will help you to focus on the positives of your training and guide you in the areas that need attention. A good instructor will always find time to have an honest discussion with you about how they see your training going, how you are developing and what you can achieve over time.

Being a good listener is a skill you can learn through the practice of martial arts, as are following instructions and both team and solo work. Your martial arts journey will require you to move forward and improve, so asking relevant questions of your instructors will be a part of your development. Asking is essential to putting the answers into practice – if you don't ask, you don't learn.

There will also be times when you are left to solve training problems on your own. For example, if you have learned five or six techniques and your instructor outlines a specific attack, it is up to you to decide which technique/s to use in this scenario. Decision making is a life skill we can all use.

Being able to share your own ideas and feedback with your group will help build your confidence and self-esteem. Never be frightened or too intimidated to answer a question with the knowledge you have at any one time. If your answer is right, that is brilliant and will help build your confidence; if it is not, then you will have learned something new. Ask questions, share feedback and have discussions with your group. It's all part of the process.

Measurable results

There is never any hiding when it comes to grading or assessments. Having to demonstrate what you have learned in front of your peers and your instructor can be daunting, but just remember that everybody is there to support you and build you up. Your instructor would not put you up for a grading if they did not think you were ready.

Having passed a grading, you will feel over the moon. Pressure can bring out the best in people.

As your chosen martial art becomes ingrained into your everyday life, you are likely to find you make time on your non-training days to fit in some additional exercises. If done in the morning, this routine development is a great way of not only progressing in your chosen art, but also setting yourself up for the day. Training after work or school will promote good sleep as the exercise will help you unwind from the stresses of the day. Either way, be sure to practise your forms regularly.

CASE STUDY – PUBLIC SPEAKING

When Richard first came to my class, he had a definite lack of confidence and self-esteem. His fitness was not great and he was really nervous on his first lesson.

In my wing chun school, it is important to make everybody feel welcome and included. A great way to break the ice is to involve the whole class in the warmup. This will require each person counting out to either a simple exercise or some basic techniques. Public speaking is one of the greatest fears that people have and even a simple request to count from one to ten can be quite daunting, but the fear loop is counterbalanced by the fact that no one wants to be the only one in class who doesn't count out.

For Richard, the fact that he was courageous enough to participate was an enormous achievement. After class, he told me it was the first time he'd spoken in a group since leaving school.

Over the coming months, Richard had a great shift in confidence. Any lingering fears he may have had of not being able to participate in discussions with a group of peers completely vanished. As Richard continues his journey with me, the shy guy with a lack of confidence and self esteem has been replaced by a confident and competent martial artist. I have spoken to him on many occasions outside of class and it always warms my heart to hear his stories of how martial arts have changed his life.

Richard has taken on a more managerial role with his employer and feels he is a better father and husband. He continues to grow and develop in many other areas of his life, not just in his wing chun.

> **TASK**
>
> Write down examples of negative mindsets you are plagued by, and then rewrite them from a positive point of view/mindset. Aim for at least five.

Summary

In this chapter, we looked at the importance of understanding your mindset and its role in your martial arts journey. Being able to spot a negative mindset or limiting belief and turn this around is vitally important. We looked at how reframing a negative mindset as a positive one can help you tackle any obstacles you face.

We discussed how personal development takes time. More often than not, faster is not better, so prepare for the long haul and learn to enjoy the process.

We touched on how you can use martial arts as a mentor and the benefits of investing in yourself. Measurable goals will be invaluable in keeping you focused in this endeavour.

4
Martial Arts Styles

With a clear understanding of the benefits of martial arts and the mindset to succeed, you're now ready to look at the different styles available to you. This chapter will explore the types of martial arts, looking at hard and soft styles and the pros and cons of each. We will also look at the rise of mixed martial arts (MMA) and how it moved from an outlawed practice to a viable and well-regulated option.

There are over 180 different martial arts found all around the world. A quick search in your local area will show you what's available near you. The decision you make on which martial art will suit your needs will be based on your current state of health, your age and, to some extent, your fitness, although any school should be able to adapt its syllabus to make it inclusive to all.

Here are some examples of the types of martial arts:

- Luta livre, a Brazilian grappling art
- Malla-yuddha, a form of combat wrestling from the Indian and Southeast Asian areas
- Nam hong son, nhat nam and qwan ki do, from Vietnam
- Niyuddha, an ancient Indian martial art
- Yaw-yan, a Filipino kickboxing martial art
- Zui quan, a Chinese style of kung fu also known as drunken fist

Of course, there are more well-known martial arts to choose from:

- Aikido
- Aikijujutsu
- Araki ryu
- Brazilian jiu-jitsu
- Capoeira
- Choy li fut
- Danzan ryu

MARTIAL ARTS STYLES

- Eskrima, arnis and kali
- Jeet kune do
- Jujutsu
- Karate
- Kung fu

This will give you a good idea of the amount of choice available. The most popular martial arts for children are kickboxing, karate and kung fu.

The martial arts actually go as far back as the first Olympic Games in 776 BC, which involved a Greek style called pankration. This combined boxing, grappling and kicking techniques.

We can arrange the different martial arts into six styles:

- Stand up and striking
- Ground fighting and grappling
- Takedown and throwing
- Weapons based
- Meditative and low impact
- Hybrid styles (mixed)

For the purpose of this overview, though, let's just concentrate on two broad categories of martial arts techniques: hard and soft.

Hard and soft martial arts techniques

In martial arts terms, a hard or a soft technique is characterised by how much force the defender uses to counter an attack. Both hard and soft martial arts have their benefits, so if you haven't decided on a style before you find your instructor, your decision may depend upon the style your chosen instructor teaches. A soft style is usually kinder on the body; there are fewer blocking force-on-force techniques and tend to be more breathing exercises and meditation. A hard style will give you lots of body conditioning and fitness which allow you to 'brush off' impacts.

As with all aspects of martial arts, Yin Yang applies to hard and soft styles, so there will be some crossover between them.

MARTIAL ARTS STYLES

I was only a few months into my wing chun kung fu journey when I was presented with a soft technique called bong sau (wing arm), which at first seemed unnatural and ineffective. How was I supposed to lift my elbow higher than my wrist while keeping my wrist on the centre line and maintaining relaxation to block oncoming punches?

Why not try it yourself? Take one arm and extend it out in front of you. Not fully; make sure there is still a bend in your arm. Imagine you are holding a small mirror in your hand; you should be able to see your reflection.

The distance between your torso and your elbow needs to be at least the width of one fist. With an upward-facing palm, make sure your hand is roughly at the same height as and in line with your nose. This is the starting position, referred to as tan sau (upward-facing palm).

To get your arm into the bong sau position, maintain your palm's current height. Keep your wrist in line with your nose, lift your elbow and rotate your palm outwards, maintaining relaxation in the hand and wrist.

Try this a few times, resetting the tan sau position, then rotating to bong sau. Does it feels awkward and unnatural? Who said martial arts was easy?

Bong sau is an intercept technique. Stick, feel, then move on to another technique. When executed correctly, it means you do not clash with any oncoming power. The rotation of your body as your arm moves into the bong sau position takes you out of the way of the direct strike, while the softness of the bong sau alleviates the incoming strike's hardness. It's a perfect example of Yin Yang at work.

Bong sau would be categorised as a soft technique because the method requires minimal force. Any movement used to deflect or redirect oncoming force is a soft technique. Other examples are:

- A slight twist or turn of the body to redirect the attacker's energy, causing the attacker to stumble
- Throwing techniques, which also use the principle of redirecting momentum

An excellent example of a soft martial arts style is wing chun kung fu.

The hard style

When a head-on force meets force, this would be considered a hard technique. It requires greater strength for successful execution than a soft technique, but a skilled practitioner will have the advantage of understanding the mechanics of a hard technique, giving them the ability to cut the strike diagonally if needed.

Examples of hard techniques are:

- A Thai boxer's low kick aimed at the leg
- A block in karate aimed at an attacker's arm and intended to cause damage
- A knee strike

Hard techniques are both offensive and defensive, and can also be used as a counter-offensive move. The use of footwork is essential, but style dependent.

Mixed martial arts

When I was beginning my martial arts journey, what is now known as mixed martial arts and the Ultimate Fighting Championships (UFC) weren't even around. There were different martial arts schools in my local area, but none offered a mixed or hybrid approach.

When it first came to the UK, MMA was deemed too violent. I remember reading an article in the *Birmingham Mail*, a local newspaper, back in 2007. The paper and the British Medical Association were campaigning to have the sport banned, and if you look back at early video footage on YouTube, you won't have too much difficulty understanding why there were safety concerns.

The bouts were more akin to street fights. There were no fundamental rules or weight class divisions; it was an 'anything goes' type of event.

As a martial artist, I can understand the wish to test skills against others, but like boxing, there needs to be some safety procedures in place. All this changed for MMA when the UFC came to the scene on 12 November 1993.

The UFC was co-created by Rorion Gracie and a promoter named Art Davie, the idea around the championship coming from the Gracie challenge.

MARTIAL ARTS STYLES

This challenge was an open invitation to other martial artists to prove the effectiveness of their Brazilian jujitsu.

UFC 1 was held at the McNichols Sports Arena in Denver, Colorado, and the first fight was between a sumo wrestler named Teila Tuli and mixed martial artist Gerard Gordeau. A real David versus Goliath match. It didn't last very long, Gerard Gordeau delivering a kick to the face. Teila Tuli lost a tooth and gained a bloody lip, face and nose, and the first match was over.

The final of UFC 1 was contested by Gerard Gordeau and Royce Gracie. Gracie beat Gordeau via submission to win the tournament, and UFC and a regulated form of MMA were born.

TIP

Being humble or quiet when you meet someone new or even in a crowd does not mean you are without power or knowledge. On the contrary – during times of crisis, look for the calmest person in the room. In the spirit of Yin Yang, calmness can cut through panic.

TASK

Can you remember the differences between a hard and soft martial art style/system?

Can you name a martial art that begins with A, W, H and J?

Summary

In this chapter, we looked at the different martial arts available to you. With over 180 martial arts worldwide, the one you choose could be dependent upon your location.

We discussed Yin Yang within martial arts, looking at a wing chun technique called bong sau in particular. Finally, we discussed MMA and how this initially dangerous area of the sport became regulated with the birth of the UFC. This was a game-changer for many martial arts and its impact is still being felt to this day.

5
The Right Martial Art For You

We have looked at the reasons to begin your martial arts journey, what you can use as motivation and whether you have any role models to inspire you. With a strong reason why behind you, along with the overview of the different types of martial arts available that we covered in the previous chapter, let's now focus on the right martial art for you.

The style you choose to learn will depend on what interests you and your overall outcome and goals. You will also need to consider what you would like to master – ground fighting/grappling, stand up and striking, etc.

There are four main categories we will cover in this chapter: Chinese, Japanese, Korean and Brazilian martial arts. We will begin by clarifying these to give you a greater insight and understanding of what each one can offer so you can decide whether it's right for you.

Chinese martial arts

When it comes to martial arts, the Chinese have a well-established and documented history, more so than any other country in the world. If you were to trace Chinese martial arts throughout the ages, you would discover descriptions going back to the Xia Dynasty over four thousand years ago.

It is believed that the Yellow Emperor, Huangdi, who ascended to the throne in 2698 BCE, introduced the earliest forms of martial arts to China. Sun Tzu's famous book *The Art of War*,[5] written during the sixth century BC, contains concepts which have helped to shape and evolve martial arts. They are used in business as well, showing how martial arts have always benefited all aspects of life.

There is a myriad of distinctive styles of Chinese martial arts, each with its own history, techniques and ideas. Kung fu is an umbrella term that covers more than martial arts; it can be applied to any study or learning that requires patience, energy and time to

---

5   Sun Tzu, (translated by RT Ames) *The Art of War* (The Folio Society, 2010)

complete. Being one of the oldest martial arts systems around, kung fu training involves a lot of variety.

Wing chun is a form of close-fighting kung fu that incorporates simultaneous blocking and defending, traps and low-level kicking. The use of sensitivity and footwork makes it an excellent all-round martial art to learn.

Here are some other common Chinese martial arts:

- Five ancestors kung fu – this Southern Chinese martial art employs five different principles and techniques
- Northern praying mantis – taken from the many martial arts of Shaolin, this attacks joints and pressure points with lots of elbows and palm strikes
- Northern Shaolin, a powerful yet soft and fluid style
- Tai chi – an internal Chinese martial art practised for defence training, health benefits and meditation
- Hung ga – a Southern Chinese kung fu style which incorporates both internal (internal energy) and external (physical) methods
- Choy li fut combines martial arts techniques from various Northern and Southern Chinese kung fu systems

- Lau gar – meaning Lau family fist, this was derived from a form of boxing practised at Kuei Ling Temple
- Fujian white crane – originating in the Yongchun county, Fujian province, white crane is a Southern Chinese martial art

Japanese martial arts

The history and development of the Japanese martial arts centre around the people living in Okinawa Islands, situated south of Japan, who were exposed to Chinese kung fu daily, mainly because of their close proximity to China. Over time, the people on this island started to develop their own fighting style and this became known as karate. *Kara* means empty and *te* means hand, so karate quite literally means empty hand.

If you were an outsider looking in at the development of karate, it would appear remarkably similar to that of kung fu, but one of the main differences is the variety of techniques. The karate system developed into a more streamlined fighting art. Another notable difference is the way in which karate is executed. Karate techniques have become a lot more linear in their approach, taking out unnecessary movements.

This is most evident when you're watching the forms. All of the karate techniques are performed with crisp snapping movements that have a distinct start and stop, which can make karate look cumbersome. When it's correctly executed, though, karate generates power that is formidable. This is one of the reasons why karate is considered a hard style whereas kung fu has styles that would be considered soft because of their continuous flowing movements.

Just like kung fu, the word karate is used as an umbrella term that encompasses lots of different subsets of styles. Here is a list of the more common subsets:

- Goju-ryu, Japanese for hard-soft style
- Isshin-ryu – founded by Tatsuo Shimabuku in 1956, this is a style of Okinawan karate
- Kyokushin – a stand-up fighting style, this full-contact martial art combines a philosophy of discipline, self-improvement and hard training
- Shito-ryu – founded by Kenwa Mabuni in 1934, this is a combination of various Okinawan schools of martial arts
- Shorin-ryu – one of the oldest styles of karate
- Shotokan – developed from a combination of martial arts by Gigo Funakoshi and his father Gichin Funakoshi
- Wado-ryu – the emphasis on striking, joint locks and throws, this is one of the four major karate styles and was founded by Hironori Otsuka

Korean martial arts

The Korean martial arts also date back thousands of years. Probably the best known is tae kwon do. *Tae* means to kick with the foot, *kwon* means to punch or strike with the hand, *do* means art or way, so its literal meaning would be the art of kicking and punching.

Tae kwon do is renowned for its jumps, spinning and fast kicking techniques. Although it is a relatively new martial art, developed in the 1940s, it relies on traditional disciplines and requires many years of practice to master. Like many other martial arts, tae kwon do has its main emphasis on speed and agility to defeat an opponent.

Some other popular Korean martial arts are:

- Hapkido – classed as a hybrid martial art, this self-defence system uses kicks, punches, joint locks and throwing techniques
- Taekkyeon – a TMA with fluid foot movements employing the use of hands and feet at the same time to cause unbalance in an opponent
- Tang soo do is based on karate with the inclusion of the principles of Northern Chinese martial arts
- Kuk sool won – founded in 1958 by Suh In-Hyuk with a wide range of offensive and defensive

techniques, this is intended to take advantage of the human body's pressure points
- Subak – bare hand techniques

Brazilian martial arts

If you know anything about martial arts and the word 'Brazilian' comes into the conversation, the chances are Brazilian jujitsu[6] will soon feature. This martial art was developed in the 1920s by Brazilian brothers Carlos, Oswaldo and Gastão Gracie, but there is an older, more traditional martial art associated with Brazil called capoeira. This originated in the sixteenth century and is martial art infused with dance, for good reason.

It is believed that capoeira was created by slaves who were taken from West Africa to Brazil by the Portuguese colonists. Because they were forbidden to practise any form of fighting, they invented an ingenious way to bypass those laws. Using rhythmic movements to disguise kicks and other techniques, they combined these flamboyant movements and capoeira came to life.

---

6   The jujitsu martial art was originally developed for samurai, Japanese jujitsu is suitable for real-life combat situations. It is often taught in a very traditional setting where discipline is greatly valued. Brazilian jiu-jitsu, on the other hand, is primarily used for sport with a primary focus on grappling.

It would be unlikely that you would confuse capoeira with any other martial art system. It is instantly recognised by its movements.

Other Brazilian martial arts include:

- Brazilian jiu-jitsu – based on ground fighting and submission holds, this is a martial art and combat sport combined
- Vale tudo – a full-contact combat sport and martial art
- Luta livre – Brazilian submission wrestling

CASE STUDY – MY JOURNEY INTO WING CHUN

I started my wing chun journey entirely by chance. I got talking to a guy at work named Dean, who was the type of guy you would hear before you saw him. He was always laughing, bubbly, friendly and humble.

During one of our chats, the conversation turned to martial arts. As soon as I mentioned Bruce Lee, Dean's eyes lit up. It turns out he was an avid collector of Bruce Lee memorabilia and was also practising the style of kung fu called wing chun. I'd never heard of wing chun. Bruce Lee, yes; jeet kune do (way of the intercepting fist), yes; wing chun, no.

It turned out that Bruce Lee first trained in wing chun before his move to America, when he created his famous jeet kune do. The fact that I could follow in the footsteps of the famous Bruce Lee whetted my appetite to find out more about wing chun, and that is how my story began.

Many years later, I now have the privilege of teaching wing chun full time in my award-winning facility known as a kwoon, a training hall for Chinese martial arts. Why not get chatting to people you know who are active or interested in the martial arts? It could be an excellent way to help you come to your decision about the right martial art for you.

Body and mind

There are many factors to consider when you're looking at learning a martial art. The state of your current health is one of these, and this could be instrumental in determining whether a hard or soft style suits you better.

Of course, you must be mindful of your fitness, flexibility and age when you're starting your martial arts journey, but neither age nor lack of fitness should be something that holds you back. If you are concerned about the impact of a martial art on your health, there would be no harm in seeking medical advice to put your mind at ease. Before you start any new physical pursuit, it's always worth having a chat with a medical professional, just to be sure you're in the right place to get going. You know your own body better than anyone else, but please be mindful that if you have not undertaken any form of physical activity for a while, you will have a few aches and pains after your first lessons. This won't last, of course.

The attitude of the person learning a martial art is also an important consideration. Determination and focus are essential as there will be challenges to overcome, so a never-quit mindset will be a significant benefit.

Just like age, disability is no barrier to studying a martial art. I have had the pleasure of teaching those with varying degrees of disability over the years, and as both people and martial artists, they always amaze me, not only with their skill, but also with their grit and determination and knowledge. Despite their disabilities, they're often the first to show up in class and among the last to leave. There are days when they come to study in obvious pain, but they put on a smile, pick up the pads and are ready to train. This willingness and dedication leads to other students looking to them as an inspiration and source of strength.

Imagine you are feeling hard done by because you have had a rubbish day. You arrive at class and the first person you see is a student with physical disabilities. They greet you with a smile, ask if they can train with you today and tell you they are looking forward to class. How do you think this would make you feel? This tiny gesture could change your attitude, give you a lift and ensure you have a great training session.

Living with any disability is hard, but I have seen first-hand what it is possible to achieve. If you have a disability, you have a couple of choices: you can look for an adaptive martial arts school or go to a regular class. Either way, the benefits you'll obtain will significantly impact your life in a positive way.

CASE STUDY – TRAINING WITH A DISABILITY

As the martial arts world becomes more inclusive, many people with disabilities do not want to learn an 'adapted' style; they want to learn the original. Why not?

I had a telephone call one day from a lady enquiring on behalf of her husband, who wanted to train in wing chun at my school. She told me he had already been training in the art for a few years, but was looking for a new school and a new challenge.

I asked if he would like to come for a free lesson as an introduction to me and the current students. Before I could take any contact details, she asked me if my studio had access for people in a wheelchair. I am fortunate enough to have a ground-floor studio and asked her about the nature of her husband's disability.

'He has muscular dystrophy,' she told me. At the time, she did not want to go into further detail about her husband's disability and said that he would explain more about it in person when he attended class.

On the day of his first session, I was at my school an hour early, making final preparations, tidying around, ensuring everything was clean before class. There came a knock at the door and there stood my new student. With my limited knowledge of muscular dystrophy and going on his wife's words on the phone, I had been expecting a person in a wheelchair. Nonetheless, I greeted him with a smile and handshake and invited him in.

He explained his condition and how martial arts had literary saved his life. He told me that his physical health had not been good when he first started his martial arts journey, but he was determined to become the best person he could be and would not let his condition stop him from training. Overweight due to lack of exercise, he was determined to do something about this. By taking things slowly, adjusting his diet, having grit and support, he was eventually able to put aside his wheelchair for his martial arts lessons.

As we continued to discuss his journey, the challenges he had faced and successfully overcome, I could not help but feel a sense of awe. While some students don't attend class because they have a slight headache or a stubbed toe, this guy, in constant pain, was looking forward to training. The fact that he was even in my class was fantastic and his story is enough to inspire anyone.

He told me he wanted to start from scratch and wished to go in the beginners' class, a humble thing for him to do as it turned out. As I got to know him better and found out more about his story, I discovered that he was a sifu (teacher) in his own right. He had his black sash and teacher's certificate.

Over the months that followed, he became an immensely popular member of the club, always first to arrive and last to leave. Having another sifu in the class was a great resource and allowed for diversity of training, making me a better teacher and the wing chun school more progressive in its approach to teaching this fantastic martial art.

THE RIGHT MARTIAL ART FOR YOU

> **TASK**
>
> Which type and style of martial art would you consider learning, and why?
>
> Write down at least five things that excite you about learning that particular martial art.

Summary

This chapter explored what could be the right martial art style for you, looking at the background of four places where martial arts developed: China, Japan, Korea and Brazil. We then went on to discuss the fact that age and physical health should never be a barrier to beginning your martial arts journey, and attitude is all important. Often the students who appear to be the most compromised turn out to be the most dedicated and become an inspiration to others.

That said, understanding your body and doing what is right for you are paramount, so take all the correct precautions to ensure your physical health is not compromised. You will feel some aches and pains after your first few lessons if it's been a while since you last undertook any physical exercise, though. That is normal and nothing to be concerned about.

6
Personal Growth And Development

No matter which martial art you choose to pursue, your personal growth and development will be assured. Exploring and understanding the type of personal growth and development you wish to achieve will be unique to you.

If you lack confidence or have low self-esteem, taking the first steps on the martial arts journey may seem daunting. Rest assured that in a short space of time, this will change and you will feel accepted, included, more confident and excited about the next lesson – as long as you have chosen your school wisely. We will look in more detail at choosing the right school in the next chapter, but before we do that, let's examine the positive changes you can expect to see in your life as a result of studying a martial art.

Martial arts and positive change

If I were to ask you why you think people take up a martial art, what would be your response? Would it be for fitness, self-defence, to meet new people or to try something new? Just think about that question for a moment; how would you answer?

When I first started my martial arts journey back in 1989, fitness wasn't an issue. Deep down, I knew my self-confidence and self-worth needed work, but I also believe that my ego had a part play. If I got into an altercation, with martial arts training, I could kick butt, right? Having the wrong attitude can get you into all sorts of trouble, so before you begin your martial arts journey, let's look at the right reasons to start and when you can expect to see the positive changes taking shape.

Personal changes may go unnoticed in the beginning as small incremental improvements only become apparent over time. These subtle changes could include waking up in a better mood, refreshed after a good night's sleep, and automatically improving your diet and drinking less tea or coffee or alcohol as your body demands healthier alternatives. These small changes may initially slip under the radar, but just imagine the feeling of wellbeing you will accumulate.

Let's say you have been training in your chosen martial art for one year. If you stop then and reflect upon your life, how far have you come? You could ask yourself what has changed personally? What improvements have you noticed?

As you get further into your journey, others may notice the changes in you first. They may comment on your air of extra confidence or how you seem less stressed and able to deal with problems in a calmer, more determined manner. Some people keep a martial arts journal or write a blog, which gives them something to look back on year-on-year to see their personal growth and development. This is a useful tool for when you hit a wall or feel stagnated in your training.

CASE STUDY - SHIFTING STUBBORN WEIGHT

Training in a martial art can give you a great perspective on your overall lifestyle. When I was beginning my wing chun journey, a guy who started at the same time was clinically obese. Although going to the gym and doing additional cardiovascular exercise, he never managed to get his weight to fluctuate.

Over the years of training, taking small steps and staying determined, he enjoyed what can only be described as a total body transformation. If anyone were ever looking for inspiration to reach their goals, then I would point them in his direction. He would explain to them how he lost almost 8 stone thanks to the study of wing chun and is now a personal trainer.

> This complete transformation was not just down to him learning martial arts; the self-awareness and growth that martial arts gave him, which made him question his lifestyle choices and habits, also played a massive part. It was a complete paradigm shift in how he approached his whole life.

As your martial arts skills increase, so will your confidence, which will allow you to do other things you have perhaps been too scared or intimidated to try. Maybe you've always wanted to climb Kilimanjaro or run a marathon for charity, or even go skydiving. The confidence that training in martial arts will give you can make you feel unstoppable.

Applying the Yin Yang principle, martial arts will also give you humility. Always approach your training or sparring partner or opponent with quiet confidence and humility. In the past, I have made the mistake of thinking I was unbeatable. Being humiliated in competition by somebody I had thought was inferior to me in both stature and skill was a lesson learned – the hard way!

Developing discipline

Discipline becomes second nature to you as you fit your training schedule around your busy, hectic lifestyle. If you commit to getting better at your chosen martial art, it will take dedication and discipline, but

PERSONAL GROWTH AND DEVELOPMENT

when you see the benefits studying a martial art gives you, that tends to be motivation enough to make sure you are ready to train on time, which leads to better discipline in all walks of life.

The word 'discipline' can have negative connotations for some people who associate it with punishment. The discipline I am referring to means self-commitment and self-dedication, which I'm sure we can all agree are positive traits.

Coupled with discipline is the development of determination. A healthy mind is essential when you're training in martial arts. It may be that you have a grading or assessment you need to prepare for, or maybe there are techniques or exercises you are struggling to master that need more practice. Having a determined mind will help you reach that goal.

Another by-product of learning a martial art is emotional stability. Being able to go into a class, completely switch off from all the daily stresses and strains and focus on one thing has a massive positive effect on your mood. Many times, students have come to me after my classes and said that the session was just what they needed after an awful day. Never underestimate the benefits of physical exercise for your mood.

Over time and with continual small steps, your personal growth and development through involving yourself in martial arts will become apparent. Always strive to be a better person today than you were yesterday. At this stage of the book, you likely have a clear understanding of the benefits of taking up a martial art and how it can have a massive positive impact on your life. A little encouragement can go a long way, so I hope this book is offering the encouragement you need and you are becoming more enthusiastic about beginning a martial arts journey.

> **TASK**
>
> What personal changes would you be most excited about seeing through your martial arts journey? List as many as you can think of and they will become a huge part of your all-important why.

Summary

In this chapter, we looked at the personal growth and development you can expect when training in the martial arts. We saw how the all-round benefits of studying martial arts led to a massive weight loss for one man, taking him from clinically obese to being a fit and healthy personal trainer.

The positive changes you can expect from martial arts training will reveal themselves over time as you make incremental improvements. It may be your friends and family will notice the improvements before you; it may be you'll gradually realise that you feel fitter, healthier, more positive and can become an inspiration for them. Think now of the positives that you expect from studying martial arts and you will have a large part of your why right there.

7
Find The Right School

Most martial arts instructors are teaching their chosen art because of the love and knowledge they want to share. I knew after only a short time of training that I wanted to teach martial arts. For me, this is my passion.

Let's now discuss the things to look out for when you're choosing where to train in martial arts, ensuring that you ask the right questions and get good value for money. Initial research will help you decide what style of martial arts you want to try, but how do you go about critiquing a martial arts school? It's time to find out.

Do your research

How many people do you know who currently practise martial arts? Chances are within your circle of friends or acquaintances, somebody will be practising. If this is the case, they are a great place to start your research. If the martial arts school they attend is good, then the feedback they give you will be positive, so ask them for their honest opinion. Is the school one they would recommend for you or your children?

Over many years of teaching, advertising and marketing, I have discovered that word-of-mouth recommendations always bring the most enthusiastic students. The prospect of training with friends or family is a great motivator. Also, while students may be looking for a great teacher, in return, a teacher is always on the lookout for great students. By great, I don't mean you need to be the next Bruce Lee; anyone with the right attitude towards their training and their fellow students is welcome.

If none of your friends or family can recommend a martial arts school, then jump on the internet and do a search in your area. Local martial arts schools will have websites and social-media platforms set up ready for new enquiries. With technology, you can even begin your martial arts journey online; more and more TMA schools, including my wing chun school, are adding details of their syllabus and training materials to their

FIND THE RIGHT SCHOOL

website for distance learning. If you are looking to learn from home, then the school's location will be of minimal importance. What is essential is the quality of the content, along with the value for money you perceive yourself to be getting.

As tempting as it may be to click on the first few results at the top of the first page of an internet search, please do not limit your choices like this. Many great martial arts schools do not have a big marketing budget and may be on pages two, three or four. Looking at student reviews is one way to ascertain the school's reputation, but be mindful of any scathing or over-critical reviews. I am aware of some martial arts schools near me that offer brilliant service to both adults and children, but due to one or two disgruntled students or a spiteful competitor, their reputation has been tarnished. Remember that there are always two sides to every story.

You may receive a flyer through the letterbox or see a poster in your local post office or chip shop. This is a favourite tactic when a new martial arts school has just opened up and is looking for students. This was how I started, canvassing my area and local businesses. I was fortunate enough to have a press release in the local newspaper – there is nothing wrong with free advertising!

If you do happen to come across a new martial arts school, this is a great time to get on board as everything there will be fresh and exciting. You also have the bonus that all the people starting at the same time as you will most likely be beginners too.

If you have children who want to start training, they may receive an after-school martial arts club flyer from their teacher. If this is the case, then the martial arts instructor will probably specialise in children's classes, but they may have classes for adults that run later in the evening. You could have a look at joining in too.

While doing your research, you will look at many websites. At this point, it's essential to remember your motivation and reasons for wanting to start or continue your martial arts journey. With your why in mind, ask yourself if the website triggers your inspiration.

A website should inform you of the club's ethos and give you information about the instructor, the times of the classes and the location. It should also have student reviews and photos to help you get a feel for the classes on offer. Nowadays, many schools offer a free trial period. Some offer one lesson, others a week or even a month for you to try the classes before you commit. Trying different martial arts styles for free is an excellent way to find the one that you enjoy the most.

If the website does offer a free trial, there's a good chance you'll need to fill out a form with your name, contact number and email address. It is always a good sign if you get a reply within twenty-four hours of submission. You may receive an automatic response saying that your details have been received. In this instance, expect a follow-up email, text or telephone call from the school. If you don't receive a follow up, maybe this isn't the school for you. After all, you are the customer and have the right to demand excellent customer service.

Whether the martial arts school has a full-time location or the classes are held in a church hall, leisure centre or scout hut may impact the days available for training. Schools running from a leisure centre or scout hut will, of course, have to fit in around the other activities at that facility. I am fortunate enough to run a full-time facility, which gives flexibility in the classes and the times I teach, but when your motivation is on point, adjusting your schedule to fit the classes in – at least one per week – should be easy. At the beginning of your martial arts journey, you may feel the need to train three or four times a week. That is great, but be mindful you do not burn yourself out. Take your time and enjoy the journey.

Both full-time facilities and those run from a leisure centre or church hall have their pros and cons. Usually, a full-time facility will have slightly higher fees, but is also likely to offer a greater range of classes and more capacity. Depending on your budget and the commitment you can make to your training, you can often choose from different plans – bronze, silver and gold packages, for example. Other schools will charge a flat fee.

Always be wary of martial arts instructors who are not prepared to tell you their prices over the telephone. It is important to know what you are signing up for before you commit. Even if you are enrolling in a free trial, ask what the fees will be once that's over and what the opt-out clause is. You don't want to find yourself automatically charged for classes in a martial art or at a school you have decided is not right for you.

When you're discussing training fees with an instructor, bear in mind that annual subscriptions, insurance and uniform may not be included in the monthly payments. Some schools will combine these into one monthly fee while others will charge separately. It's always best to suss this out right at the start.

Your first session

Attending your first training session is a big and important step that should not be underestimated. Plucking up the courage to attend can be a stumbling block for many; I have had countless telephone conversations with potential students who are enthusiastic to attend classes, and then don't turn up. When I get in touch with them the following day, they usually say much

FIND THE RIGHT SCHOOL

the same thing – their apprehension, nerves, anxiety, fear got the better of them. I have even spoken to a new attendee while they were sitting in their car in the car park, unsure whether they had the courage to take the step through the door.

This feeling is totally normal. Anyone who has ever tried something new has faced this type of apprehension. Taking yourself out of your comfort zone is never easy, but it's so beneficial, and believe me, you will feel great about yourself once you've done it. Be brave and enter your martial arts school with a smile, even if this is simply hiding your nerves.

When you arrive for your first lesson, expect to be greeted warmly by either a senior student or the instructor. Any decent instructor will have a clean, crisp uniform and a big smile. I would recommend that when you attend your trial class, you participate rather than just observe. I know it is much easier and less intimidating to sit and watch, but you will not get the feel of the club or the martial art unless you take part. Participation is key, so take yourself out of your comfort zone and join in.

CASE STUDY – YOU'RE WELCOME!

One day, Emily finally walked into my club. I say 'finally' because I had spent the best part of six months in discussion with her. She was unsure whether trying martial arts again was for her. Her own personal experience at a badly managed school had left a lasting impression.

Going to another martial arts school that taught wing chun, she had not been made to feel welcome or appreciated as a student. She was left in a small group with other beginners and not given any actual instruction throughout the class. 'Stand over there and practise basic punches' hardly counts as suitable guidance for someone new to the sport and is no way to treat a potential member of a martial arts school.

When Emily finally made it through the doors of my school, I could sense her apprehension, lack of confidence and low self-esteem. I can understand anyone's anxieties at entering a new environment, but anyone who attends my training sessions will be made to feel welcome and included. It needs to be so at the school you choose.

After only a few months, Emily had become a model student, friendly and respectful. Gone were the nerves and low self-esteem. She has made many lifelong friends and is an integral part of our current wing chun development programme.

The way other students act at the school you choose, whether they're senior, intermediate or beginners, should be exemplary. A martial arts school is a place for discipline and, more importantly, respect. Abusive language must be forbidden and the other students, especially the senior ones, should show a lot of humility. Martial arts brothers and sisters tend to become firm friends so a bit of banter is bound to happen, but

FIND THE RIGHT SCHOOL

any good martial artist will also show respect, especially in the company of guests.

If you are attending a children's martial arts class as a parent, look for an atmosphere that's lively and fun. Expect the other children to be a little boisterous and excited as their love for their martial arts training comes to the fore.

Your first impression of the school, the instructor and the other students will have a massive impact on your decision regarding whether this is a place you wish to train. If you are going to commit to learning a martial art, you will be spending many hours in the school, so make sure it is right for you. The owner or primary instructor should take time to speak with you, answer any questions or concerns you may have and make you feel at ease. After all, they would like you to spend your hard-earned money and valuable time at their club.

Depending on the first impressions, you may wish to sign up for a school after your initial lesson. If that is the case, brilliant! You'll have found a good match – as long as you have taken the advice in this chapter and made a considered decision. Do not feel pressured into signing up or agreeing to terms that you are not happy with. The club has to feel right for you; martial arts is about sharing knowledge, not hard sell. If you feel pressured or that the place doesn't sit right with you, simply leave. You are under no obligation to stay.

CASE STUDY – FOCUS AND DETERMINATION

A new student was enthusiastic to attend training with me, but he wanted to know if he could come along with a friend of his. When two friends come and train together, it is usually because one is feeling nervous and needs a bit of moral support and back up.

When the two friends arrived and were settled in, the lesson started. I made a point of taking the time to train with them, which is something I do with any potential students as it is vitally important. To make them feel welcome and included, I give them plenty of time and attention. Everyone was a beginner at one time and none of us get a second chance at a first impression.

After the two friends' first session, they told me they were both keen to continue training, which is always nice to hear. The more engaged and eager of the two told me he was currently playing badminton twice a week and was curious to see how much physical activity he could take on before he couldn't do any more. I admired and enjoyed his keenness.

Over the next few months, both friends continued training, but eventually, the less engaged one told me he could no longer commit to training. I remember wondering at the time if that would mean the other would stop coming as well. Little did I know.

This man has strong determination and focus, facing challenges involving a physical and mental element head on. He is now my longest-serving student and assistant instructor and has the nickname of Terminator.

After your trial lesson, if you feel you need time to think about whether to join or not, picture yourself going back to the school next time. Do you get feelings of excitement or nervousness, anticipation or dread? If your feelings are positive, this could be the right place for you; if not, perhaps try a few other places.

Another way to judge how you feel about your first lesson is to think about what you would write if asked to do a review of the school. After only one lesson, would you recommend the school to your friends? Would your review be full of positive or negative words? Again, if you have more negative things to say than positive, it's probably best you go elsewhere, but if you are raving about how good you feel, how brilliant the class was and how you can't wait to go back, telling friends and family about this amazing martial arts school, this is a good sign that you have found the right place for you to begin your martial arts journey.

Empty your cup

If you have never trained in martial arts before, going to your first class will likely be exciting and nerve wracking in equal measure. There is nothing wrong with feeling like this as a beginner, but if you have studied martial arts before and are now taking up a different style, it is essential to empty your cup, ie leave all your old learnings and preconceived ideas at the door. Otherwise, it can be extremely easy to take them into the new system.

Not emptying your cup when you start something new can lead to confusion, frustration and a slower learning pace. Have discipline and humility. It's important that preconceived ideas or previous martial arts experience don't stand in your way. Don't expect your new studies to be identical to the old ones.

CASE STUDY – THE CUP OVERFLOWETH

Once upon a time, there was a wise Zen master. People travelled from far away to seek help. In return, he would teach them and show them the way to enlightenment.

One day, a scholar came to visit the master for advice. 'I have come to ask you to teach me about Zen,' the scholar said, but after many hours of conversation, it became apparent that the scholar was full of his own opinions and knowledge. He interrupted the master repeatedly with his stories and failed to listen to what the master had to say.

Finally, the master suggested that they should have tea. He poured the scholar a cup, but when the cup was full, he kept on pouring until the cup overflowed on to the table, the floor and eventually the scholar's clothes.

'Stop!' cried the scholar. 'The cup is full already. Can't you see?'

'Precisely,' the master replied with a smile. 'You are like this cup – so full of ideas that nothing more will fit in. Come back to me with an empty cup.'

Stay humble, open yourself to new ideas and be willing to change your preconceptions. My martial arts background before wing chun was kickboxing and muay Thai. In kickboxing, like any martial art, movement is critical. You shift your weight and move on the balls of your feet, just like a boxer would, and this is remarkably similar to muay Thai and many other martial arts. Footwork is a vital skill to master, but it is vastly different in the wing chun system where you move in small steps, almost flat-footed with the weight distribution slightly over the heels.

If you have never done martial arts before, although this footwork may seem strange, it is fairly easy to pick up. If you are coming from another martial arts discipline, though, learning it can be challenging. It certainly was for me when I started on my wing chun journey.

If I'd gone into every lesson saying, 'This footwork makes no sense' or 'I can do better than this', my progress would have been sporadic and I probably would not have stuck to wing chun. I had to leave my previous knowledge in the back of my mind to allow the new ability to take hold. Creating neural pathways in the brain and allowing ideas to form is the most efficient way for this to happen.

Think about the last time you learned a new skill. At the beginning, you may have been completely rubbish at it. At this point, you were unconsciously incompetent

– you didn't know what you needed to do, let alone have the skill to do it. Over time and with continued practice, you mastered the skill. You became unconsciously competent, meaning you could do the task without even thinking about it.

You may want to try some online training before you commit to a martial art. If that is the case, all you need to do is schedule a little bit of time each week. Above all else, whatever art you choose and however you decide to train, stay humble, open yourself to new ideas, have a willingness to learn and empty your cup.

CASE STUDY – MAKING THE TRANSITION

Mike, one of my longer-serving students, has been training with me for the past seven years. He is a qualified black-belt instructor in his own right and has a karate and aikido background. I recall having the initial conversation with Mike and asking his reasons for wanting to add wing chun to his already impressive martial arts knowledge. He responded with this.

'Walking into a martial arts club is a big step for some people to take. Luckily for me, I knew someone who also wanted to try the wing chun system, so the much-needed support was there. Taking the first steps on your own can be daunting.

'From a martial arts perspective, I was attracted to wing chun because of its flow of movement, the independence of each limb to subdue an opponent and it looks cool. What did I get out of my first lesson?

FIND THE RIGHT SCHOOL

'I found like-minded people who were welcoming and helpful with a willingness to share. What this demonstrated to me on a personal level is always to take the first step.

'Be brave and ask yourself, "What is the worst thing that can happen?" If you don't like it, move on. You will find a club that is right for you. Overthinking and fear of the unknown are not the easiest things to beat, but you will thank yourself if you do.

'If you already have a martial arts background and are considering taking up a new style, there will be challenges to face. As the story of the overflowing teacup explains, you need to be empty before taking in more knowledge.'

I asked Mike how he found the transition.

'I have been training in wing chun for about seven years and I believe I am still in the transition phase, and will never leave it. This is not a bad thing, because learning in this art allows me to reflect on the deeper meaning of my earlier training. There are lightbulb moments of realisation about how my other training can be applied in new situations. Another art brings this to my attention.'

Already having a martial arts background, Mike struggled to get to grips with some aspects of wing chun at the beginning of his journey.

'The basics are always the most difficult things to move across the arts. I found myself focusing on techniques, but the foundations like stance and weight distribution were wrong. The important thing is to clear the mind of previous experience. Take in the new teaching fully.

'This does not mean you lose your previous knowledge, but don't compare how one art would deal with a situation with another. Neither approach is wrong, but each one is built upon its basics. If you develop a good foundation, your actions will be effective. I still need to work on this aspect of my wing chun development.'

Finally, I asked Mike if he had anything else to add.

'Take that first step on your journey. It will be worth it as you learn new skills, meet like-minded travellers and undertake an activity that supports a healthy mind and body.'

Going the distance

Many adults will have a story to tell about how they tried something when they were younger and wish they had kept it up into their adult life. The 'something' may well have been martial arts.

Why do people give up on something they later claim they enjoyed? When somebody new attending my school tells me they used to train in their younger years, I'm always curious about what stopped them from continuing their training. The reason they give can probably be found on this list:

- They played football/rugby/other sports and wanted to dedicate their time to that.

- They were meeting women/men and embarking on new relationships.
- They enjoyed clubbing and going out for a good time too much.
- Work got in the way.
- They lacked the self-discipline to continue.
- They thought they knew it all and had no further need for training.

When I question them further and ask if they regret not continuing their martial arts journey, the answer is always yes.

If you trained in martial arts in your younger years, why did you stop? Would you like to start again? The good news is it's never too late – the best time to do that is today, whether you choose the same style as before or a new discipline.

I'm not saying starting again is easy; the obstacles of your ego, pride, age and lack of motivation can be significant ones to overcome. Even though you are aware of the benefits that training in a martial art can bring you, starting again on a new journey can be a challenge.

Being able to empty your cup is especially important. If you go into your training session with the attitude that you know best, the chances are you will not enjoy it and quit. Do not get me wrong: sharing your knowledge and experience is OK, but if there is no room left in your mind for new ideas and concepts, you will be defeating the object of starting again. Never allow your ego to get in the way of your training.

> **TASK**
>
> How do you think you could mentally prepare yourself to go to a new martial arts class?
>
> Do you think you have any reservations that would stop you attending your first session? If so, what steps could you take to overcome these reservations and doubts?

Summary

In this chapter, we covered the importance of finding the right school for you. Ideally, the school's location will be convenient for you, but if you decide on a martial art that isn't taught locally, you have the options of travelling or practising remotely online.

Full-time martial arts centres will usually charge more than a martial arts school in a sports hall or scout hut. Either way, though, the warmth of the greetings you receive and your first impressions are excellent indicators of how well the school is run. Pay attention to how you are treated. How does the instructor make you feel? Do they make time to speak to you? Remember you are a guest at their class.

The other students are also good indicators of whether this martial arts school fits your needs. For example, are you made to feel included? What is the atmosphere of the place? Can you see yourself training there again?

Finally, no matter what your previous experience or preconceived ideas of martial arts may be, empty your cup before you attend a new school.

8
Investing In You

Overcoming barriers and finding ways to encourage yourself and others on your martial arts journey are vital skills to learn. The personal empowerment that comes from the martial arts may not be evident for all to see in the beginning, but it will become obvious. If you can encourage others when they need some help, you will be helping yourself as well. Support is a two-way street.

We all have days when things just don't seem to go right and the only thing we're looking forward to is getting back into bed. When was the last time you had a day like that? Sometimes, the last thing we want to do when we get home is go out again. The little inner voice is telling us that it's OK to miss today's lesson, we will only be learning the same thing we did in the previous one. We promise ourselves that if we don't go to class this evening, we will go three times next week. I'm sure everyone has been there.

The question of missing a few lessons over the course of a year doesn't amount to much if your attendance is usually on point. It only becomes problematic when you are finding more and more excuses as to why you cannot attend class. Procrastination is the killer of dreams.

Life is full of ups and downs, challenges and obstacles to overcome, and the same can be said when you're learning a martial art. Any excuse will slow down your progress. If you are not moving forward, you're stagnating or moving backwards. It is easy to think that you will make up for lost time and train twice as hard on the next lesson, but this rarely happens.

In this chapter, we will look at the importance of making a commitment to invest in yourself and attend class regularly. There are plenty of things that you can do to encourage yourself and others.

Forming habits

As adults, we often wish that we didn't have to go to work, wash the dishes, walk the dog, go shopping, go to the gym, etc, but we also know we have to. No work equals no money; no washing of plates, then there's nothing to eat off; no dog walking leads to an overactive dog; no shopping, no food. No martial arts training means no benefits to mind or body.

Time management is important in many walks of life, as is forming good habits. If you or your children are regularly skipping your martial arts sessions, you are inadvertently forming a new habit pattern, replacing the practice of training with not showing up.

It can be particularly challenging to convince a child that continuing with a martial art will benefit them not only now, but into their teenage years and beyond when you're competing with the lure of playing on a gaming console or watching the latest series on Netflix. Remember, though, that as a parent, you are responsible for your children, physically, mentally and emotionally. Do not give in to the protests, either from your children or, if it's yourself you need to motivate, your inner voice. The PC, TV, Xbox, PlayStation will still be there when you and the children return from training.

Keeping to a routine of martial arts training is just like going to work/college/school. It is essential to your continual development, not only within your chosen martial art discipline, but also your life. If you find yourself trying to justify why it is OK to miss a few training sessions, remember the reasons why you started training in martial arts in the first place. Think about what motivated you and reflect on the progress you have made. If you keep a martial arts journal, looking back over this can be a huge help in reinvigorating you and reigniting your training passions. Even if life circumstances change and you can no longer attend classes, would that stop you from being able to train remotely via an online learning platform?

Here are a few tips that can help get you back on track if you're feeling discouraged in your martial arts journey:

- Ask yourself if you're being too hard on yourself, expecting too much too soon. If this is the case, review your training goals and perhaps ease them a little.

- Are you tracking your progress regularly? Doing this can make you realise just how far you have come.

- Do not be too hard on yourself if you do have to miss a day or two's training from time to time, but be mindful that you are not creating a new habit for yourself.

- Regardless of where you are on your martial arts journey, do not compare yourself to others, even if you see people who started training after you progressing more quickly. Focus on yourself; do not let others deter you from your goals.

- We all struggle with motivation from time to time, so why not engage with friends or family to see how they can encourage you to continue your training? Better still, chat with your instructor and fellow students. They will likely be delighted to help.

- Remind yourself how elated and energised you feel after each class, and focus on the great times you have had and the lessons you've learned.

- Have you taken on too much training? Reducing it for a while can help get you back on track – ask your instructor for guidance.

- If you have skipped a few weeks, but are determined to get back to training, don't focus on the time you've missed. Instead, focus on the future and the classes you will attend.

- How about rewarding yourself at the end of each month of full attendance? A new outfit, a massage or taking a friend or partner out for a meal can be a great incentive.

Remember that your martial arts training is a journey so enjoy the process. Set goals for the future, but focus on the present. Do not let the time and effort you've put into your training to go to waste.

CASE STUDY – FATHER-AND-SON TRAINING TEAM

When Steve, one of my best friends, got in touch and expressed an interest in training with me and bringing along his son, I was really excited. I'll admit, though, I felt a little apprehension too.

You are likely to be familiar with the concept of never mixing business with pleasure, and this was what initially worried me. You may recall that at the beginning of my martial arts journey, I was persuaded to try kickboxing by a friend called Steve. This is the Steve who now wanted to train with me – no pressure there, then. Would teaching a friend and his son be a good idea? As it turned out, I had nothing to fear.

The reason Steve wanted his son to start training was because the boy was one year away from secondary school and Steve thought learning martial arts would benefit him as he progressed into the unknown. As well as the physical and self-protection side, this would give a boost to his self-confidence.

This father-and-son team training together has been great. Steve himself said, 'It is fun, learning with my son, seeing him progress and his confidence growing.'

With learning anything new, there will always be challenges. For Steve and his son, the basic wing chun stance and vertical fist punches were the hardest parts to master, but training together, they were able to encourage each other. Better still, if one had experienced a bad day and was reluctant to attend training, the fact that they'd be letting the other down served as a great motivator.

When I asked Steve why he continues to train and assist in my school, he said, 'For me, wing chun is more than a martial art. The more you do it, the more you realise there is so much to this system beyond just punching.'

Overcoming barriers

There can be times in your journey when you feel like there are barriers and obstacles holding you up. These can come in many different shapes and sizes, but being aware that they're there can help you either overcome them or avoid them completely.

At the beginning of your martial arts journey, you're likely to feel enthused to start something new. As the excitement and novelty of the new activity begin to fade, keeping your motivation high is vitally important. A regular schedule will be an essential part of this.

When I was learning kickboxing, I was regularly awarded the 'Student Most Attended' prize. Because martial arts is so much a part of me, without training, my day does not feel complete.

As your martial arts skills develop, regular attendance at your classes will maintain what you have already mastered and improve the areas in which you are lacking. If you are swapping training hours for other perhaps less-physical activities, then you need to regain the motivation you had in the beginning. One way of doing this is to monitor your activities over the course of a week to see where you could be more productive with your time. Have you let bad habits slip into your daily and weekly routine? Are you getting enough sleep and feeling refreshed in the morning?

Getting good-quality sleep is vitally important, not only for your physical and mental wellbeing, but for your daily life. If you have plenty of energy left at the end of the day, making time for training is easy. Tiredness will not become a barrier.

Monitor your sleep patterns over the course of a few weeks by either jotting down the hours you went to bed and when you woke or using an app to track this. It will give you an overall picture of your sleeping habits and you'll be able to make adjustments to your routine if needed. Smart watches also have a function for tracking the times you were awake during the night and the quality of your sleep.

Of course, there will be some of you who suffer from insomnia. As with anything, my first advice here would be to consult with a medical professional to make sure there is no underlying health issue causing your insomnia, but there are also a number of things you can try to help yourself.

Often, people lie awake at night with their brains racing over the things they have to do next day. A great help can be to 'brain dump' by listing out everything you have achieved during the day that has just passed, then plotting your tasks for the next day. Write it all down, get it out of your head before you settle down to sleep. Mastering the art of meditation can also be a great help to quieten your thoughts.

Make sure you eat your last meal of the day well before bedtime, and avoid caffeine and alcohol in the hours leading up to going to bed. Some people mistakenly think alcohol helps them sleep; you may fall asleep rapidly after a drink or two, but your sleep won't be good quality and the likelihood is you will be awake again in the early hours. Daily exercise helps no end, but not just before bedtime as you don't want the endorphins racing when you're trying to sleep. If you're training regularly in your chosen martial art, this is likely to help you sleep soundly at night and wake the next day refreshed.

Avoid blue light as much as possible, especially in the evening. Blue light sends messages to your brain that it's work time and you should be awake. It is all around us these days, emitted from TV screens, mobile phones, computer monitors and even digital clocks. Perhaps invest in an old-fashioned wind-up clock if you like to have one in your bedroom (the ticking sound can be wonderfully soporific). You can also invest in blockers to clip over your glasses if you wear them, or you can wear them like sunglasses to reduce the stimulating effects of blue light.

Routine is important to a good night's sleep. If you go to bed and get up at the same time every day, your brain will learn when it can expect to settle down to sleep and when to wake up. Tempting though it may be to have a lie in on weekends or holidays, it won't help you feel less tired in the long run.

It's not only lack of quality sleep that can make you feel tired, though; did you know that dehydration can also cause fatigue? Whether you work in an office, have a job that is more physical or are still at school or college, it is vitally important to stay hydrated. If you are feeling thirsty, you are already dehydrated. The current guideline in the UK is to drink around 2 litres of water a day.

Not only is remaining hydrated beneficial to your body, it will stop you from feeling sluggish, especially after lunch. Again, you can make a note of your water intake or use an app to do it for you. You may be surprised how little water you drink.

I'm sure you know that nutrition is important to your wellbeing. When you hear the word 'diet', you may envisage living off salads, counting calories and not being able to have any nice foods for the rest of your life. There is nothing wrong with having a salad from time to time, but if that is all you ever eat, your mealtimes will rapidly become boring.

The food you put into your body ultimately gets used as fuel. If it is of low quality and high in fat and simple carbohydrates, you will get a rush of blood sugar when you've just eaten. This feels great for about half an hour, then fatigue and tiredness set in. Maintaining a healthy and balanced diet will not only benefit your health, it will also help maintain your energy levels throughout the day.

You may be at a point in your training where you feel you should have progressed more and you lack the skills to continue. This could simply be due to the skill you're learning. If you are good with your hands, for example, and your current curriculum is all about footwork, kicks and movements, this will inevitably take you longer to master. The frustration you feel can be a barrier to continuing your martial arts journey, so be mindful of this. Perseverance is key. Remember that without practice, you will never overcome this barrier and master the skill.

As you progress through your training programme, there will come a point when you have to put your knowledge into physical action, whether this is sparring, application work or scenario-based drills. If you feel a little apprehensive or unsure of your skills, the fear of having to spar or fight, even in a controlled environment, can be a barrier. Please remember that your teacher and your fellow martial artists are not there to hurt you or humiliate you. Everyone who attends a martial arts school is there for their own development. Do not let fear get the better of you.

Fear is a psychological barrier. If it occurs for you, it needs to be addressed with your instructor or a senior student. No one will ever force you to participate in an activity that you do not wish to do.

Finally, the weather is a common barrier to attendance. If it's cold and wet outside and you've only just got home where it is nice and warm, it can be a real challenge to get changed into your training gear and go back into the cold and wet. This situation can be even worse if you rely on public transport or a lift with someone else to get to your training destination.

It can also be a problem when the sun is shining. Your neighbours may be having a barbecue or your friends calling you to go out for a few drinks. There's nothing wrong with missing a training day here or there to socialise when the weather is good or if there is a major sporting event on the TV, but remember that once a positive habit has been broken, it can be a challenge to start again. Students who have trained with me for years have given up, and when I enquire as to why they have stopped, they reply that they have fallen out of the habit of training. With some encouragement and a gentle reminder of why they first started their martial arts journey, their passion for training can often be re-ignited. So it can be for you.

How martial arts empower you

If you were to take an honest look at yourself in the mirror, what would you see? Would the person looking back at you be someone you love and admire, or would you notice only flaws and defects in the reflection?

A martial arts journey will take you on a rollercoaster of emotions. There will be days and weeks when everything just clicks and there will be other times when nothing seems to go right. This is to be expected and is all part and parcel of the journey.

To be empowered should be one of the goals of not only martial artists, but every human being. To be in control of one's life ultimately leads to freedom. As you progress in your martial arts and look back on the journey, you will notice aspects of your life that have changed or are changing for the better. That's a great way to feel empowered.

TIP

If you can walk away from an altercation, then do so. It is more empowering to wake up the following day with damaged pride than a damaged body, or even worse, not wake up at all.

An increase in your self-esteem is usually detected by others first. Changes in your behaviour or how you apply yourself to specific tasks or situations become apparent to them while slipping under your radar. This is because the incremental changes over the weeks and months of your training are so small, it is only when you are called upon to act in a certain way that you realise you are different now, on both a personal and professional level.

The type of training you undertake will over time impact your physique and your health. I am not saying that after six months you will have a six pack, but your strength, stamina and flexibility will have improved. If your training is coupled with an awareness of diet and staying hydrated, your energy levels will also be on point.

As with the changes to your self-esteem, the improvements to your physical health can also be subtle. Not getting out of breath when walking up a few flights of stairs is a great example. Maybe you can now run to catch the bus or the train, something you could not have done before you started training. These changes to your body are a direct result of your martial arts sessions.

Your body will constantly adapt to any physical exertion that you put it through. The longer you continue your martial arts journey, the more apparent this will become. Seeing people in their fifties and sixties diving, rolling and being thrown like they are teenagers is marvellous. The conditioning of their bodies, fitness and stamina is a sight to behold. It's one of the greatest inspirations to me.

Depending on where you are within your learning cycle, you will inevitably make mistakes. Sometimes they will be small, but sometimes you will get something completely wrong. No matter how hard you try, you just cannot seem to 'get' it.

Practising and making mistakes, then practising again and again until you eventually get it right is a skill worth learning. Not only will making mistakes keep you humble, but it will also make you realise that there is always something new to learn. You cannot get everything right first time; practice makes perfect.

Without making mistakes, you will never progress. Each time you do something incorrectly, you have learned how not to do it. Eventually you will get the technique correct and happily move on to the next one. If you execute the technique perfectly every time, you will quickly become bored and pursue something different.

All the hard work you put into your martial arts training will be noticed by members of your family and your work colleagues. As a result, you could become an inspiration to them. This doesn't necessarily mean they will take up martial arts, but they may enquire about your fitness or diet. This may encourage them to take a look at their own lifestyle and make small adjustments. How great would it be if a loved one or friend's health and fitness improved because of the example you have set?

> **TASK**
>
> If you are the type of person who finds it easy to form new habits, do you feel confident that you could form a good training habit when it comes to your martial arts?
>
> Conversely, if you are the kind of person who finds forming positive habits a challenge, what steps can you put in place to help you facilitate good habits when it comes to your training?

> Score yourself on a scale of 1 to 10, where 1 is poor and 10 is excellent, in these areas:
> - The quality of your sleep
> - Drinking enough water
> - Eating a diet that is 'on point'
> - Investing time in yourself

Summary

We have covered a lot of subjects in this chapter. The main point that I would like you to keep in the front of your mind is the importance of sticking to your habits even when life throws you a curveball. Consistency is paramount in so many areas of your life, so keeping to a routine of martial arts training is vital to your continual development, especially in the early stages of your journey. There are many obstacles that could get in your way, but being aware of these obstacles is the first step to overcoming them.

Remember that without making mistakes, you will never progress. Make the mistakes, learn from them and move on. You never know, you may be inspiring someone by your consistent actions and the empowerment you are gaining from them.

9
Laying The Foundations

Understanding the learning process and not getting frustrated with failure or slow progress develops character and determination. Solid foundations are vital for any martial art, but you need to be aware that building them takes time.

When it comes to learning, everyone has their preferences. Often, people naturally focus on the practical side of martial arts education, which makes perfect sense at the beginning of their journey, but understanding the physical characteristics of a martial art will help with the cognitive processes and build familiarity with the moves, putting into perspective the learning journey ahead. The physical side is actually only a tiny part of learning a martial art.

TAKING THE MARTIAL

If you have an insight into how you learn and the stages of the learning process, this helps you if you get frustrated with your progress. When you plateau, you feel unsatisfied, knowing that you have come so far, but you are not there yet. Knowing where you sit on the learning process will help you push through and keep your learning on track.

TIP

When you're learning martial arts, focus on the areas that are your weakest. The things you are naturally good at will always be there. Build upon your weakest points so that they become assets, not liabilities.

The four stages of learning

Whenever you are learning a new skill, there will always be a curve. The stages of learning have been studied in great detail since the 1970s, started by Noel Burch's introduction of the conscious competence ladder.[7] Understanding and applying this concept to your own learning is a great way to appreciate the process – something we all have to do when learning a new skill.

---

[7] L Adams, *Learning a New Skill Is Easier Said than Done* (Gordon Training International, 2021), www.gordontraining.com/free-workplace-articles/learning-a-new-skill-is-easier-said-than-done, accessed 15 December 2021

LAYING THE FOUNDATIONS

The four stages of the conscious competence ladder relate to us evolving from not even knowing we're incompetent at a skill to being able to perform it as second nature. Let's apply this learning model to a new student starting on a martial arts journey.

Stage 1 – Unconscious incompetence. The student does not understand how to do something or necessarily recognise a given technique's complexity in sufficient detail. At this level, they may openly deny the usefulness of the skill, even thinking it is impossible to learn. With good coaching and encouragement, this stage will soon pass.

It is important at this stage for students to recognise and accept their own incompetence and see the value of the new skill they are trying to learn. Learning takes time, so a good teacher who encourages and corrects them in a positive way is a great help.

This stage must be acknowledged on a conscious level before the student moves on to Stage 2, otherwise excuses and/or boredom stemming from a lack of understanding and increased frustration will stop them from learning the skill completely, probably leading to them giving up. The length of time any individual spends in this stage depends on the strength of their why coupled with their willingness to learn. Having a good teacher who understands unconscious incompetence, including the frustration and inevitable mistakes that come with learning a new skill, is an enormous help at arguably the most important stage of learning.

Stage 2 – Conscious incompetence. At this stage, the student will not fully understand how to do a technique, but they will recognise the insufficiency of their skill and the value of the technique.

Understanding why you are trying to do something shows that you are developing a martial arts mindset. At the consciously incompetent stage, you will be aware (conscious) that you cannot yet execute the technique, this fact being a massive step forward from unconscious incompetence. It is important to note that mistakes are integral to the learning process at this stage. These mistakes must be observed, discussed with your instructor or senior student, corrected and practised, ironing out any faults. Again, with encouragement and positive, constructive feedback, you will successfully conclude this stage of learning and progress on to the next.

Stage 3 – Conscious competence. The student understands or knows how to do something well, but demonstrating the skill requires concentration. Simply adding a new element, sequence or routine will have the student really focusing and concentrating to incorporate it, and can start the process from Stage 1 again. Even asking the student to explain step-by-step what they are doing can cause them to freeze or become slightly frustrated as they have to process the steps internally before expressing them in words.

An instructor adding additional techniques or sequences at this stage will observe the student going through the unconsciously and consciously incompetent stages again, albeit quickly as they incorporate the new steps into an already known sequence. They will then become more comfortable as they get back to being/feeling consciously competent at the task at hand.

Stage 4 – Unconscious competence. The student has put in so much practice that the technique has become second nature to them and they can perform it easily. Any additional elements can be assimilated, adapted and refined almost at will. As a result, the student can perform the technique while executing another task or even multiple tasks.

To put this into the context of an example most adults will recognise, cast your mind back to the first time you got into a vehicle with your driving instructor. Can you remember how overwhelmed you were with all the things you were expected to do?

On my first lesson, I was unconsciously incompetent. I had trouble processing which pedal was which, let alone how to operate them with my feet while taking control of the steering wheel with my hands. Then there was having to pay attention to the other drivers on the road, using my mirrors and indicators and staying within the speed limit. All this while listening to instructions and not stalling the car.

Now when I get into my vehicle, I turn on the ignition and drive. All the practice I have had over the years has made me unconsciously competent.

TIP

When a person can explain a technique and answer questions in a simple manner, only then are they truly unconsciously competent.

Building a solid foundation

Now that you have a clearer idea of how you learn, it is time to start your martial arts journey. Building a solid foundation is key to your future success, so if you are currently trying out different styles to see which one suits your needs, then please come back to review this chapter when you have made the decision. If you have already decided which type of martial arts system is for you and you are ready to commit to your learning or have already begun, it will benefit you to refer back to this chapter from time to time as you progress.

No matter which type of martial art you have chosen, whether it be stand up and striking, ground fighting and grappling, takedown and throwing, weapons based, meditative and low impact or MMA, your training will begin with the mastery of the foundation/basics. The importance of a solid foundation cannot be overstated. It is even referenced in the Bible:

> 'Therefore everyone who hears these words of mine and puts them into practice is like a wise man who built his house on the rock. The rain came down, the streams rose, and the winds blew and beat against that house; yet it did not fall, because it had its foundation on the rock.
>
> 'But everyone who hears these words of mine and does not put them into practice is like a foolish man who built his house on sand. The rain came down, the streams rose, and the winds blew and beat against that house, and it fell with a great crash.'[8]

The principle of building a house on a solid foundation can be applied to your martial arts training. If you take the time to understand, develop and become unconsciously competent at the basics of your chosen martial art, then you will have a solid foundation on which to build.

I have observed over the years of teaching at my wing chun school that some people wish to rush the basics so they can move on to what they see as the more advanced techniques. There is nothing wrong

---

8   Matthew 7, verses 24–27, New International Bible

with wanting to progress in your art, but do not mistake quantity for quality. Developing your foundation will pay dividends in the near future.

No matter the martial arts style that you have chosen to pursue, it will have its own movements. These will include the basic stance. For example, in the wing chun system, the basic stance (yee gee kim yeung ma) is a foundation from which all the other stances will stem. The stance itself, especially at foundation level, is not designed for fighting or movement; the position of your feet, the pulling in of your knees and your weight distribution are the points to concentrate on. Because of the way the legs bend, while a student is practising this stance, they're also building strength in their legs.

As a student progresses through the wing chun system, this basic stance becomes less intensive and their movements become easier and freer. Without understanding the stance's importance or balanced movement, though, they will find their footwork will forever be tied and have no flow. It is imperative to master the basic stance and build a strong foundation.

Let's take a look at the basic karate stances. In karate, a beginner/a white belt would be expected to learn five basic stances (dachi):

- Ready stance (heiko dachi)
- Short fighting stance (han zenkutsu dachi)

- Long forward stance (zenkutsu dachi)
- Horse riding stance (kiba dachi)
- Sumo stance (shiko dachi)

Understanding the importance of each of these stances and when they should be used will help the student build their foundation. In karate, there are other stances that will be introduced as the student progresses through the system, but these five basic stances will be used throughout their entire journey.

In the Korean martial art of tae kwon do, depending upon the activity, a student could use one of several different stances. If you were to observe the form competition of Hyeong, you would see a whole repertoire. Each of the stances is critical for balance, precision and good technique. The more advanced techniques cannot be executed if the foundation is weak.

If you choose to study one of the grappling or throwing arts such as jiu-jitsu, aikijiujitsu or aikido, the basic stance would be different again. I have simply added some examples to show that each martial art is based on its own set of principles.

The importance of the fundamental principles of your martial art may only become apparent after you have trained for a while. In the beginning, each of the movements may seem cumbersome or unnatural, but as time progresses and you go through the learning stages until you become unconsciously competent, you will realise the importance of a strong foundation. Until you master the basics, do not even attempt the more advanced techniques.

Repetition is the mother of skill

Once you have mastered the basics and foundations of your martial arts style, then comes repetition. If you have ever watched a child learning to walk, you'll know it would be difficult to count the number of times they failed and fell over. Once they took the first few steps and found their balance, walking became second nature to them, and they can now do it over and over again, honing their newfound skill. Then comes running, jumping and skipping, but only once the foundation of walking has been laid.

The same would apply to a child learning to talk. They start with mimicking certain sounds before gaining an understanding of and being able to form simple words such as 'dad' or 'mum'. Regardless of the number of times they have to practise, the young child will repeat the process until they get better and start to grasp the complexities of language. Even children who live in multilingual households can assimilate and differentiate between each language with ease once they have mastered the basics.

TIP

Many things can be achieved with small steps, motivation and dedication. All you need is your strong reason why.

No matter where you are on your martial arts journey, remember that repetition is paramount in your progression. I had to apply this principle to myself during the Covid pandemic of the early 2020s. I could have closed my martial arts school down and not given any consideration to my students, but I realised the importance of regular repetition and training. This is the only way to maintain the same level of skill at the very least.

I'm sure you have heard that you never forget how to ride a bike. As much as this is true, the last time I rode a bike, it took me a few minutes to readjust my balance and feel confident and in control. When I observed others who ride a bike as part of their daily lives, I could clearly see the difference. The same will be true for anybody coming back to their martial arts after a break. They won't ever forget the martial arts training they have received in the past, but just like a tool that is never used, rust can set into their skills after a time of inaction.

Why is repetition so important? Neural pathways communicate information from one area of the nervous system to another. These pathways consist of neurons connected by dendrites and are formed in the brain based on our unique habits and behaviours. The connected neurons process the information that we receive, enabling us to interact and experience emotions and sensations.

In an article written by Alison Pearce Stevens, you can find out more about the process of neural pathways and how learning rewires the brain.[9] In the learning process, some of the brain's nerve cells change shape or even fire backwards. This all sounds complicated, which it is. Delving into neural pathways and the workings of the brain is not an easy subject, so let me illustrate this in a different way.

Imagine you are driving along a dirt track. There are rocks, bumps and potholes – plenty of obstacles. As you continue along this path, it widens to become a lane made of asphalt. There are fewer defects and you enjoy a smoother journey. Further on, the path widens again to become a two-lane carriageway, and so on until it's a six-lane super-motorway.

Your martial arts skills can be likened to travelling along that initially bumpy path. The more you practise something, the stronger the neural connection in your brain will become. Conversely, the less you practise, the weaker they will be. This ties in perfectly with the four stages of learning.

---

9 A Pearce Stevens, 'Learning rewires the brain', *Science News for Students* (2014), www.sciencenewsforstudents.org/article/learning-rewires-brain, accessed 2 May 2021

Quality over quantity

There will be times in your martial arts training when no matter how hard you try, progress seems slow or you appear to have plateaued. Even when you become unconsciously competent at a skill, there are always little tweaks to make for improvement. In the case of wing chun, a great example is being able to relax under pressure (for example an attacker coming in with force or multiple assailants at the same time). When you get to this stage of your training, you need to focus on effort, not the outcome.

> 'I fear not the man who has practiced 10,000 kicks once, but I fear the man who has practiced one kick 10,000 times.'
> — Bruce Lee

As the great man's words show, even though you may perceive your progress to be slow when you focus on one aspect of your training, the constant and consistent practice will serve you well. The emphasis on effort over outcome really stands out for me. If you focus each week on your effort in specific areas of your whole life, not just your martial arts training, how much do you think you could achieve? If you're determined, both physically and mentally, to achieve a set goal daily, weekly and monthly, you will progress a lot faster than if you're jumping from one goal to another without achieving the best possible result in any of them.

In wing chun, the vertical fist punch is one of the first techniques a student will learn. The punch itself is straightforward. Raise your arm to the centre of your chest with your fist in a vertical position and punch until your arm is extended. It is a simple enough technique to master, but if you only focus on the end point, then it won't really matter how you get your vertical fist into the extended centreline position. You could take your hand out to the side of your body, down to your waist, above your head, and then with a circular motion place your fist in the correct finishing position. Instead, your attention needs to be on effort to make sure your fist does not deviate between the starting and end point and travels along the shortest path, in this case a straight line.

This simple example illustrates the importance of focusing on effort rather than outcome, but of course, learning martial arts does have an outcome. In fact, it has many positive outcomes, but if you only focus on the outcome, you will miss the fun of learning a new skill and overcoming the challenges you face.

If you look at learning a martial arts discipline, these are a few of the positive outcomes you can expect as a result of your focus on effort:

- You'll be a better, more well-rounded person.
- You'll enjoy enhanced life-skills (placing emphasis on values and attitudes).

- You'll increase your self-confidence.
- You'll understand effort and reward.
- You'll improve your focus and determination.
- Teamwork and getting on with others will become second nature.
- Respect for others and yourself will also become natural to you.
- You'll be an inspiration to all and a role model for the younger ones.

Martial arts employs techniques that build strength, endurance, posture, balance and coordination. No matter what your reason is for starting martial arts training, applying yourself with maximum effort, you will see progress more quickly than those looking at the ultimate outcome they want to achieve without any focus on the effort they must put in to get there. Remember, even when you have been training for many years, there are always things to improve upon. This can only be done with the correct attitude and effort.

TIP

Train hard, but stay focused and humble. There is no room in the martial arts for ego and pride.

> **TASK**
>
> When you come to learn a new martial arts move, write down as many reasons you can think of as to why repetition is vitally important.
>
> Do you think it is better to master a small number of techniques or be average at lots of different techniques?

Summary

In this chapter, we had a look at the important aspects of learning. The four stages of learning apply not only to martial arts, but to embarking on anything new. Understanding these stages will give you an insight into where you are in the goal of becoming unconsciously competent.

We then discussed the importance of building a strong foundation when it comes to your training. In martial arts, this foundation tends to start with the basic stance. Repetition is critical to making sure you are unconsciously competent at the foundations before you move on to further your skills, and even at the unconsciously competent stage, there is still room for improvement. Never make the mistake of thinking you know it all. Consistency is an important concept in life as it is in martial arts. If you don't use a skill, it will become rusty and dull.

LAYING THE FOUNDATIONS

Understanding how your brain creates new neural pathways is also useful in life and training. Always strive for quality over quantity; better to excel in one thing than be average in everything you do. Focus on your effort and you will achieve the outcomes you desire; focus only on the outcomes and they will remain dreams.

10
Advance In Your Art

In this chapter, we will examine how you are likely to progress through your chosen martial arts system. Whichever art you are considering or training in, there will always be gaps that need filling and new things to learn.

The route to advancement

Advancement in martial arts can take many forms. Not all learning in the arts has to be physical. How you develop will depend upon which type of martial art you have chosen.

Let's recap on the main styles of martial arts:

- Stand up and striking
- Ground fighting and grappling
- Takedown and throwing
- Weapons based
- Meditative and low impact
- MMA

Many of these martial arts styles fall into four categories: Chinese, Japanese, Korean and Brazilian.

Your chosen martial art and your instructor's past and how they were taught will have a significant bearing on how you learn and the ethos of the school. I know of instructors who spent many years in China or Japan being taught their chosen style, which has had a significant impact on the way they run their school and the traditions they favour.

If you've only just begun your martial arts journey, your advancement will be progressive. You will feel that you have many years of learning ahead of you. If you have been training for a good few years and feel that you need to delve deeper into the system, then there will be other aspects of martial arts that you can consider. As with any journey, new pathways will open up and opportunities will present themselves.

If you become curious about the deeper side of martial arts, a lot will depend on the type of training you are doing. When I was learning wing chun kung fu, my instructor's main emphasis was on the external physical techniques, rarely looking at the power of breathing or internal energy. I only became more aware of these when I dived further into my chosen kung fu system, but some of the deeper side may already be part of your training regime. Your martial arts instructor, who is there to facilitate your journey, can point the way and guide you, but ultimately this is your journey. Only you can decide which path you will take.

Don't get me wrong: you do not have to go into the deeper side of martial arts. If the training you are receiving satisfies your mental, emotional and physical requirements, that's fine. On the other hand, if you feel that learning and exploring more is what you need, then there is more to explore. If your martial art does not incorporate pressure points, for example, then this is an area that you could take a look at once you have become competent in your current style. Trying to mix and match martial arts systems and styles can become confusing if you are new to the arts.

If you have ever watched a martial arts movie or the older James Bond films, you will likely have seen the karate-type chop to the neck. If so, you will already be familiar with pressure points. Any strike directly to the carotid artery can dramatically change the blood flow, causing a knockout or worse due to the sudden drop in blood pressure. Pressure points are located all around the body. If you strike one correctly, you can cause immense pain or immobilisation.

Looking at other martial arts systems and approaches to certain aspects of the training is not disrespectful, as long as you do not force techniques that your instructor has not shown you on to others in your class. Doing so would be a sure-fire way to get yourself ejected from your martial arts school.

Breathing and meditation

The power of breathing has fascinated me since I almost drowned when I was seven years of age. I guess the need for air was great for me at that time. Here, I've grouped breathing and meditation together because I have found that they are closely related.

Chi or qi gong is an internal process with external movements, which means it can get mistaken for tai chi. If you break down the words, *chi/qi* means life force, *gong* is the term for work or to gather, so put together, *chi/qi gong* means working with your inner being.

Tai chi was initially developed as a martial art in thirteenth-century China, but is now mainly used to restore energy levels and improve balance, strength and flexibility. No longer a fighting martial art, tai chi is practised around the world as a health-promoting exercise.

What is the difference between tai chi and chi/qi gong? If you think of qi gong as a movement, you do it for a specific reason, whereas the tai chi form is a flowing sequence of moves that work on the entire body. You can regard qi gong as the practice of coordinating body posture and movement with breathing and meditation for health and martial arts training purposes.

If you were to lay out all of the veins, arteries and capillaries in one adult human end-to-end, they would stretch about 60,000 miles (100,000 kilometres). The effect of controlled and deliberate breathing has been gaining popularity over recent years. The benefits of yogic breathing (pranayama), often performed in combination with meditation or yoga and some martial arts, are of great interest for many in the health profession, and studies have shown yogic breathing's effects.[10, 11]

The Ice Man Wim Hof's breathing method with the use of cold exposure is well worth a look.[12] I have

---

10   Qing Wu et al, 'Effect of voluntary breathing exercises on stable coronary artery disease in heart rate variability and rate-pressure product: a study protocol for a single-blind, prospective, randomized controlled trial', *BMC* (2020), https://trialsjournal.biomedcentral.com/articles/10.1186/s13063-020-04402-2, accessed 15 December 2021
11   MA Russo, DM Santarelli, D O'Rourke, *The Physiological Effects of Slow Breathing in the Healthy Adult* (NCBI Resources, 2017), www.ncbi.nlm.nih.gov/pmc/articles/PMC5709795, accessed 15 December 2021
12   Wim Hof Method Breathing: www.wimhofmethod.com/breathing-exercises, accessed 15 December 2021

been practising the Wim Hof method for around eight months.

As with all new physical practices, speak with your doctor/medical professional before including breathing methods as current medical conditions may need to be taken in to account.

Body conditioning

Depending upon the type of martial arts training you are doing, you may come across body-conditioning exercises, although this tends to be something that only a few hard-core martial artists practise. These exercises usually involve hitting objects with your hands, knuckles and shins to condition you to give and take hard blows.

The type of body conditioning can vary from style to style. When I practised kickboxing and muay Thai, I was advised to roll milk bottles or a rolling pin up and down my shins to help with conditioning. It is not something I would recommend.

There are schools of kung fu that practise iron-palm training. This training involves hitting a canvas bag filled with either sand, smooth pebbles or ball bearings. When done consistently, this will help toughen the bones of the hand, but martial artists who practise iron palm need to make sure they use an excellent liniment before and after training. This liniment is called dit da jow or fall hit wine.

A dit da jow recipe is usually passed down from teacher to teacher (sifu to sifu). It helps speed up the healing process after heavy impact on a wall bag or after iron-palm training. I am lucky enough to have a unique iron-palm dit da jow recipe that is both organic and vegan.

The use of dit da jow is not limited to martial artists with impact injuries. I know acupuncturists who use it on their patients to help relieve many ailments. On a personal level, family members who have suffered joint pain and arthritis have gained relief from using dit da jow daily.

If you would like more information on dit da jow, please visit my dedicated website www.ditdajow.co.uk

Practise your forms

I have added this section towards the end of the book for a good reason. As you become better at your martial art and more new and exciting techniques dominate your training, you may start to believe it is pointless to keep going over your forms. This is not a belief you want to cling on to. Why? Let's see, shall we?

In the wing chun system, the first form is called siu nim tao or the little idea. This form teaches you to focus on one point of movement at a time. For example, if you are moving your arm from a low position to a high one, you would focus on your elbow's tip, pushing your forearm forward.

I have applied the siu nim tao principle to focus on each aspect of my life, family and business. If I try to focus on more than one thing at once, I will achieve nothing. It's linked to the principle of focusing on effort rather than outcome that we looked at in the previous chapter.

The importance of practising basics and dedicating yourself to mastering your forms is a lesson in humility that can easily be overlooked. No matter where you are in your martial arts journey, learn to appreciate and master your forms. If the martial art you are practising does not have a set routine like a form, review and become a master at the basics. Remember when we discussed the four stages of learning? The more times you go over your basic movements, the more they will become ingrained in you.

CASE STUDY – STARTING ANEW

When Keith began training at my school, he initially came with his daughter and I was unsure if he would stick it out. Keith had a background in other martial arts and found learning a whole new style a challenge.

ADVANCE IN YOUR ART

I asked him what had made him look at wing chun and he said that he needed a martial art that was not going to cause any more wear and tear on his already aging body, but one that would be effective. Keith had also been dormant for many years.

The transition into a whole new (for him) martial arts style took him a little while. After the first class, he had decided the wing chun system was right for him thanks to the tuition he had received from the helpful and friendly students in the class, but the most difficult part was grasping the simple and effective techniques involved within the system. He continually found himself trying to overcomplicate the moves, but it wasn't long before he came to realise the benefits of practising his forms. Having got the basics on point, he could then build on them and make progress.

> **TASK**
>
> Write down as many benefits as you can think of if you were to practise meditation or chi gong every day for thirty days.

Summary

In this chapter, we covered the advancement of your martial art, looking at additional aspects you could add in such as pressure-point training or breathing and meditation techniques. We also looked at the importance of never forgetting the basics as you advance.

Continuing to practise your forms is essential, and forms also play a part should you transition to a different martial art. Never try to overcomplicate things. If your chosen martial art doesn't include forms, then concentrate on the basics. This initial work will never let you down as you advance, but you will pay a price if you neglect it.

11
Martial Arts In The Modern Age

Until the birth of MMA, anybody who practised in a martial arts system seemed to have a slight air of mysticism around them. This fantasy was probably greatly exaggerated by the silver screen. Unfortunately, this led to some martial artists thinking they were invincible. Nowadays, the chances are you know somebody who practises or has practised martial arts before and the air of mystery has dissipated somewhat.

There is nothing wrong with looking and being confident, but there is a fine line between confidence and arrogance. I've seen a few people take a beating because of arrogance. It's a harsh lesson to learn.

If an experienced martial artist were completely taken by surprise and hit with a weapon or a punch to the back of the head which rendered them unconscious, no amount of training would help. What martial arts training can help with is situational awareness. Next time you are out in the city, for example, look around you. How many people are entirely oblivious to their surroundings? You are likely to be surprised at the number of people wandering around as if in a daze, looking at a mobile device and not paying attention to the world around them.

Then put yourself in the mindset of the 'bad guy' looking for an easy target. Would you consider attacking the person with both hands free whose mobile devices are safely stashed in their pocket or bag while they're completely aware of their surroundings? Alternatively, would you choose the person with no situational awareness who's completely distracted by their mobile device while carrying bags of shopping and wandering around without a care in the world? Which one would you consider to be the easier prey?

Of course, you're not going to attack either of them – I hope! Remember, though, that a career criminal is also looking for easy targets, and they do have malicious intent.

Fight, flight or freeze

When you are in the early stages of your martial arts training, it is doubtful that you will do much scenario-based ambush training. In fact, combat or ambush training may not be part of the curriculum at all, but this doesn't mean that if you were attacked, your martial arts training would not come into play. The neural pathways developed in the stages of learning would kick in, especially when you have been training for a while. This is why it is always important to practise the basics and your forms.

During the stress of an attack, your fight, flight or freeze instinct, inherent in humans since prehistoric times when our ancestors had to make snap decisions upon which their lives quite literally depended, will naturally kick in. The last place you want to be is in freeze mode. Think of a deer caught in the headlights of an oncoming vehicle. That's what I'm talking about.

If you are attacked, you need to get into fight mode as quickly as possible. Failing that, flight mode will remove you from the perilous situation. Your body will release chemicals to aid you in this, delivering a massive shot of adrenaline. Whether you have experienced a similar situation before and have the requisite neural pathways in place will profoundly affect what happens next.

CASE STUDY – A TERRIFYING ORDEAL

Hattie had been training with me for ten weeks or so. As a group, we had been working on scenario-based training which involved being approached and attacked near a wall. The attack would come in the form of either a punch, kick or grab. There are lots of different permutations to this drill, as I'm sure you can imagine.

As an instructor, I wanted to make sure everyone was comfortable with the drill and felt competent in its application. Hattie seemed happy with what she had learned. Then one week, she wasn't at training. She hadn't missed a class before, so this was out of character.

The following lesson, she told us what had happened to her.

'There is a good reason why I wasn't at the lesson last week. While I was on my way to training that evening, walking to the bus stop as I always do, I was thinking about how we should be aware of our surroundings and what is going on around us. Well, this advice probably saved my life. At the very least, it saved me from something dreadful happening to me.

'I was waiting to cross the road when I noticed a white van slowing down and the door opening. As I turned my head to look at what was happening, a guy reached out and tried to grab me to pull me into the van. I initially froze and time seemed to go in slow motion.

'After what seemed like ages, my first reaction was to punch the guy square on the nose – there was a cracking sound and he shouted out in pain. The van driver accelerated away really quickly and it was all over.

'I was shaken and people around me approached to see if I was alright. I was still in a state of shock, so I went home and reflected on how things could have gone so differently had I not put into practice what my wing chun training has taught me.'

At my club, we have a saying: 'I would rather know it and not need it than need it and not know it.' This saying took on new meaning for many at the club after what happened to Hattie.

When the hormone adrenaline is released into the body, some critical things happen to you. These include:

- Increased heart rate
- Increased blood pressure
- The expanding of the air passages of your lungs
- The redistribution of blood to your muscles
- Enlarging of the pupils of the eyes
- An alteration of the body's metabolism to maximise blood-glucose levels, especially for the brain

In a nutshell, adrenaline helps the body move more quickly, but the effects can negatively impact you if you've never experienced them before. I have known people mistake the feeling for fear.

When your body is in fight, flight or freeze mode (when you either stand your ground, run or do nothing), it may eject fluids. I have witnessed a doorman who was new on the job urinate when he first got into an altercation. As you can imagine, everybody took the piss! As part of your martial arts training, it is beneficial to understand the chemical reactions that happen within your body under the stress of a fight or an attack so you are prepared for this effect.

Scenario-based training

Whatever martial art you study, you need to know the difference between a tactical and a technical technique. If you are familiar with the famous crane kick that Daniel LaRusso used to beat Johnny Lawrence in *The Karate Kid*, this would be considered a technical kick. Standing on one leg with the other leg raised and both arms in the air would look very peculiar if you were trying to replicate this during a street fight or ambush, though.

When you are practising your martial arts forms, or even going through kicks, punches and blocks, there is nothing wrong with doing some talk-through scenario training. If you have never done this type of training before, it may feel alien and even somewhat counterintuitive initially, so let me expand upon this idea.

Imagine you are standing by a park bench waiting for a friend. Somebody approaches the bench and takes a seat. There is no indication that this person is a threat, but suddenly they lunge towards you, trying to attack you and take you to the ground. How would you respond?

The type of training you do and how you initially see the threat scenario play out in your mind will determine how you respond, so a great way to break down the scenario would be to narrate yourself through the whole process. Talking through the scenario, aloud or in your mind, indicates how you would react.

After the first run-through of the scenario, you may find yourself grappling with your attacker on the floor. Not the best outcome. Replay the scenario over again. You need to break it down in to sections to see if you can pick up any cues along the way. What can you look out for that indicates the attack is about to happen? Over time, you will discover evasive actions to get a more favourable outcome.

When I first tried this solo scenario-based training, I wasn't convinced it would have any benefits, but thanks to the four stages of learning, with each iteration of the scenario, different ideas, techniques and foot movements came into my mind. Each of these made me more aware and able to deal with the threat.

Scenario-based training is even better if you have a partner to go through the scenario with you. What you identify when you're doing scenario-based training are the techniques that work for you and those that do not. Understanding what tools you have to call upon during times of stress is vitally important and could quite possibly save your life.

Knowing which techniques work for you and which do not is one aspect of technical and tactical training. If you can subdue an opponent using only three moves, this is tactical. If you subdue the opponent using fancy and flashy techniques, this takes longer, runs the risk of not working and adds an unnecessary level of technical difficulty.

Discipline, respect and responsibility

Discipline, respect and responsibility are essential in your personal development and your martial arts school. In Western society, though, the importance of showing discipline and respect for your chosen martial art can lack significance.

As a martial artist, you must uphold your school's traditions and be mindful of the responsibility that comes with wearing its logo and colours. As an extreme example, let's say you were out shopping and you saw an argument between a man and woman. It's nothing physical, but it's extremely loud and aggressive with insults being thrown. Imagine you then notice one of the people involved in the argument wearing a logo for a local martial arts school that proclaims it to be 'The home of discipline, focus and respect'.

Do you think that this would be an appropriate advertisement for the club? Worse still, imagine if the logo belongs to your club and you are also wearing the same logo. Do you think that anyone witnessing the argument may tar you and your martial arts school with the same brush? The reputation of a club can take years to build and a few seconds to destroy.

As part of your personal development and your martial arts journey, and depending upon the reasons you have decided to train, you'll need to focus on aspects of your personality. You may be a person who takes responsibility seriously. You have no problem with respect, but perhaps your discipline is an area that needs improvement. Alternatively, it could be a combination of the three things. You will know deep down what areas need improving. Just be mindful of your behaviour at all times.

To put into perspective the fact that as martial artists, we are all responsible for upholding the good reputation of our club, let's look at another example. If you see individuals all wearing the same football shirt on their way to a match, do you automatically think they will have an enjoyable time? Do you believe they are football hooligans looking for trouble? Many people who are not followers of football themselves, but have seen footage of so-called fans causing trouble all around the world may assume the latter, even though the likelihood is most of the fans only want to enjoy a day out and hope their team will win.

Just like the football fans, your behaviour will reflect either positively or negatively on your martial arts school. Be aware that your behaviour could be judged at home, work or school. As your confidence and self-esteem grow, be mindful that you do not allow yourself to become arrogant or cocky.

If you have chosen a more traditional martial art to learn, the chances are that your instructor will make clear the discipline, respect and responsibility that you must adhere to. If, on the other hand, you have chosen a less traditional style or MMA, then it is your responsibility to make sure you do not bring any dishonour on to your school.

The branch of wing chun I belong to is part of the Ip Man lineage. There are traditions and specific ways that we all need to adhere to during training sessions. Some small examples would be always bowing when entering or leaving the training area, addressing the teacher as 'Sifu' and bowing to our kung fu brothers and sisters. Refraining from the use of foul language during training, not chewing gum and making sure our uniforms and footwear are clean and presentable are also ways to show respect. They may sound simple, and they are, but you'd likely be surprised how many people think it is OK to turn up for training with dirty footwear or creased clothes.

Before his death, Grand Master Ip Man wrote a code of conduct.[13] This can be seen on the wall of the Ving Tsun Athletic Association in Hong Kong. He wanted to remind students that the learning of the wing chun system was more than just fighting.

The code of conduct incudes:

- Stay disciplined – act ethically as a martial artist
- Be courteous and righteous – help the society and respect your elders
- Love your fellow students – be unified and steer clear of conflicts
- Limit your yearnings and pursuit of bodily pleasures – uphold the proper spirit
- Train conscientiously – maintain your skills
- Learn to develop spiritual harmony – refrain from arguments and fights
- Remain disciplined – conduct yourself ethically as a martial artist

---

13 D Knight, *Wing Chun Code of Conduct* (Wing Chun Association, 20 July 2012), www.kwokwingchun.com/about-wing chun/ip-mans-wing chun/wing chun-code-of-conduct, accessed 15 May 2021

- Practise courtesy and righteousness – serve the society and respect your elders
- Love your fellow students – be united and avoid conflicts
- Limit your desires and pursuit of bodily pleasures – preserve the proper spirit
- Train diligently – maintain your skills
- Learn to develop spiritual tranquillity – abstain from arguments and fights
- Participate in society – be moderate and gentle in your manners
- Help the weak and young – use martial skills for the good of humanity
- Pass on the tradition – preserve this Chinese art and rules of conduct

Whichever martial art you choose, do your best to remember this code of conduct throughout your daily life. You represent your martial arts school, so remain humble, focused, disciplined, respectful and continually train diligently.

Martial arts have so much to offer every individual, I wish that the practice was part of every school curriculum in the Western world. Suppose the martial arts were practised daily as part of either a mindfulness or physical-education lesson. All students would learn discipline, respect and responsibility and the world would improve tremendously.

> **TASK**
>
> Write down how important you think situational awareness is when it comes to your own personal safety.
>
> Review what you have written. Are there any aspects of your situational awareness that you will change?
>
> As your own safety is your responsibility, are there any other areas you need to change or be more mindful of the next time you are out and about?

Summary

This chapter has covered a lot of information, so if you need to re-read and digest it more fully, please do so.

When you understand why a career criminal is looking for easy targets, you're more likely to make sure you and your loved ones are not on their list. Your safety is your responsibility. Let me say that again.

Your safety is your responsibility.

Couple this knowledge with situational awareness and you may get out of a potentially dangerous situation before it has even begun.

Adrenaline and its effects on the body are essential to understand. Knowing that your heart rate and blood pressure will increase when you're under threat will make you more focused. Adrenaline helps the body move more quickly, but be mindful not to mistake these feelings for fear.

Scenario training and drills have an important part to play in your regime. The same goes for talking yourself through a scenario. Although you cannot get a 'full' adrenaline hit in this way, talking through the steps will help should you need to call upon your training in a violent encounter.

Responsibility comes with wearing your martial arts school's logo and colours. Always be mindful of your conduct as your behaviour will reflect on your school's reputation. Although Grand Master Ip Man's code of conduct was designed with wing chun in mind, you can take the principles on board no matter the style of martial arts you are practising.

Conclusion

As you have just finished reading this book, your head is probably full of ideas. You're likely to be excited by the prospect of finding the type of martial art that will suit your needs and personal development. Perhaps you're already wondering where to begin.

If you are ready to begin your martial arts training, you need to make sure you have a strong why behind you. Remember that the reason why you start training must be compelling enough to keep you going should your motivation wane. Making a note of your progress in a journal or diary can also be beneficial.

TAKING THE MARTIAL

Let's take a brief look back at what we have covered in the book. In Chapter 1, we discussed the motivation that you need to begin your journey. You can look to others to inspire you, both people you know and famous martial artists such as Bruce Lee. Every journey will have its ups and downs and highs and lows, so it's wise to remember the Yin Yang principle where fine balance is paramount. Everything has an opposite, just as night follows day.

We discussed the obvious and the less-obvious benefits of studying martial arts in Chapter 2. We looked at how martial arts can shape and inspire you to become the person you truly want to be, and how consistency is vital for anyone to change a habit. We learned how any regular exercise brings health benefits, but if you couple this with martial arts training, you also gain flexibility, stamina and endurance as well as mental focus, energy and an overall feeling of wellbeing.

The mental health benefits of martial arts are often overlooked, but we discussed them in Chapter 2. We discovered that even simple breathing exercises can lower your heartrate and stress levels and improve your mood.

In Chapter 3, we looked at mindset and the important part it will play as you consider your martial arts journey. Limiting beliefs can become a barrier not just

CONCLUSION

for martial arts study, but also in other aspects of your life. We then explored alternative mindsets and how a change of thinking can alter the approach you are taking with great effect.

Any personal-development programme takes time to develop new skills and habits, establish ideas and mould you. Taking your time is part of the process; faster is not always better so learn to enjoy the process. There are benefits in investing in yourself.

In Chapter 4, we discovered that there are over 180 different martial arts found all around the world and how we can arrange the martial arts into six different types: stand up and striking; ground fighting and grappling; takedown and throwing; weapons based; meditative and low impact; and MMAs. We explored the differences, the Yin Yang between hard and soft martial arts techniques. We also had a look at the reasons why MMAs were initially banned in the UK until the birth of the UFC had a massive impact on the martial arts world.

Chapter 5 discussed the right martial art for you. We looked at Chinese, Japanese, Korean and Brazilian martial arts, then discussed the fact that neither age nor fitness should be a barrier to you starting your martial arts journey. Many people are now training with a disability too.

In Chapter 6, we looked at the personal growth and development you can expect from training in a martial art. We examined the actions to take to ensure a clear understanding of how a martial art can have a massive positive impact on your life.

Making the decision to begin a martial art is exciting, but you need to find a school and a style that suits you. We discussed this in Chapter 7, discovering that many schools offer taster sessions free of charge. Only by attending classes can you find what is right for you, but you can do some initial research by speaking with your friends and undertaking internet searches.

Training fees and other costs are things you need to look into during this research – sometimes the most expensive isn't necessarily the best. Expect to feel included and welcome in a class. Finally, if you have a martial arts background and you're thinking of taking up a new style, we looked at the importance of making sure your cup is empty and you don't let your old learnings interfere with your grasp of new concepts.

The focus of Chapter 8 was investing in you. We looked at encouragement, forming positive habits and remembering that martial arts training, like life, is a journey. Keeping to a routine is just like going to work/college/school. We also looked at overcoming barriers, concluding with how the

CONCLUSION

martial arts empower you to become an inspiration to others.

In Chapter 9, we took a look at the importance of laying strong foundations before you progress in your martial arts journey. Building solid foundations is vital for any martial art. We looked at the perseverance and dedication it takes to master martial arts skills, understanding the learning process so as not to get frustrated with failures or slow progress. When you're learning martial arts, focus on the areas that are your weakest so that they become assets, not liabilities.

Depending upon the current stage of your martial arts journey, your speed of progress could be relatively quick or slowing down. Remember that you will never stop progressing, even if you seem to have plateaued, as long as you continue training. In Chapter 10, we discussed adding more depth to your training, such as a study of the power of breathing and meditation. Pressure-point training could also be an additional skill set to learn. We looked at how dit da jow helps with the healing process if you are practising the iron-palm system and the importance of practising your forms daily.

Finally, in Chapter 11, we discussed martial arts in the modern world. We looked at how scenario-based training can develop your neural pathways so when you are faced with a stressful situation such as an attack, you have a good chance of coming out of it unscathed. We also examined your responsibility as a martial arts practitioner to respect yourself, family, friends and martial arts school.

Now that you have reached the end of this book, I hope you are inspired to take up martial arts. The lessons you will learn about yourself, life and what you can accomplish will all manifest when you start this fantastic journey. Do not worry about your past or your age or your ability – the right time to start a martial art is now.

I would love to hear from you, especially if you have taken inspiration from this book and subsequently started your martial arts journey. Please get in touch via sifu@wingchunhalesowen.co.uk. I look forward to hearing from you.

If you are interested in the wing chun system and would like to try out the eight essential training drills you need to know, then head over to my portal at https://wingchunonline.thinkific.com to get these lessons for free.

Martial arts have given so much to my life and I want to shout about it from the rooftops. This was my motivation behind writing the book. My wish is that everyone could experience what martial arts have to offer. I would love all schools to teach them as part of their curriculum.

I wish you every success on your martial arts journey.

Sifu Alan Bagley

Acknowledgements

You can achieve so much with the right backing and encouragement. I would like to thank Steve, my brother from another mother. Without your friendship, support and guidance throughout the years, I do not think I would be where I am today. True friendship really does last a lifetime.

An enormous thank you to Mike, Paul and Charlie for giving up your time to offer support, constructive criticism and feedback. Your insights and encouragement helped shape this book and your help is very much appreciated.

To my martial arts teachers and instructors over the years, thank you for dedicating your life to martial arts. Keep doing what you love to do and inspire a future generation of martial artists.

And finally, to all my students, past, present and future. Every person who has come into my life via my school or at tournaments and seminars has taught me lessons about myself, my teaching and my own personal development. You have all helped shape me into the instructor I am today. Teaching martial arts is my passion and it is a privilege, one that I have dedicated my life to. Thank you.

The Author

Sifu Alan Bagley is the chief instructor at an award-winning martial arts school in Halesowen and has been in this privileged position since 2013. Having been involved in martial arts since 1998, he has a wealth of knowledge and experience which he shares generously during his teaching. He won the award for Best Traditional Chinese Martial Arts School in the West Midlands in 2020.

Growing up in a working-class family, Alan was encouraged to learn a trade. He became a qualified electrician, but he was never truly happy with just 'working for a living'. With an interest in the mind sciences, he has studied Neurolinguistic Programming to master-practitioner level and spent many years as a clinical hypnotherapist. He has always had a fascination for personal development and how the martial arts can help with this. Alan believes that martial arts and personal development go hand in hand and the arts can not only become a great source of motivation, but facilitate the development of many aspects of life.

Sifu Alan Bagley has worked with martial artists on the mental and psychological side of their sport both pre- and post-fight. He loves to inspire others and see them pick up the mantle of personal responsibility, watching as they evolve, change and grow.

Get in touch with Sifu Alan Bagley and find out more about his work via:

- www.wingchunhalesowen.co.uk
- www.alanbagley.com
- www.facebook.com/wingchunhalesowen
- www.youtube.com/c/WingChunKungFuLtdHalesowen
- wingchunonline.thinkific.com

www.ingramcontent.com/pod-product-compliance
Lightning Source LLC
Chambersburg PA
CBHW060658100426
42735CB00040B/3037